Understanding the Kingdom of God

GEORGIA HARKNESS

Understanding the Kingdom of God

ABINGDON PRESS / Nashville

UNDERSTANDING THE KINGDOM OF GOD

Library of Congress Cataloging in Publication Data

HARKNESS, GEORGIA ELMA, 1891-
Understanding the kingdom of God.

Includes bibliographical references.
1. Kingdom of God.   I. Title.
BT94.H34   231'.7   74-10809

Reissued 2005 by Abingdon Press

MANUFACTURED BY THE PARTHENON PRESS, AT
NASHVILLE, TENNESSEE, UNITED STATES OF AMERICA

To my friend and former pastor Dr. Pierce Johnson, now teacher of religion and chaplain at the University of Puget Sound, I am much indebted for reading the manuscript and making many useful suggestions. My present pastor, the Reverend James Dallas, has also read it, and his words of encouragement have been most helpful. Such leadership with participation in a church that is very much alive keeps me from despairing of the future of the churches in this time of great need of what the churches can contribute to our world.

Contents

Introduction

Why another book on the kingdom of God? Are there not already many of these on the library shelves? And is not this the most controversial subject in Christian theology, on which anything one says on a level beneath the surface will call forth disagreement? Granted. Yet it still seems to this author that there is a place for another book on this theme.

There is general agreement that the kingdom of God is at the heart of the message of Jesus. Try to extract it from the words recorded in the Synoptic Gospels as spoken by him, and nearly everything else goes with it. People may differ as to how to combine the apparently contradictory things on this subject ascribed to him, but nobody who reads the New Testament can doubt that the kingdom was at the center of the thinking and speaking of Jesus.

This fact alone should make the kingdom of God a matter of perennial importance. But in our time we can add the fact that while the secular world tends to look with suspicion on virtually every other element in Christian belief—the existence of a personal God, the nature of man, the relevance of the church, sin and salvation, the future life, the Trinity—Jesus himself is not in question. He is the center of faith and loyalty not only in the Jesus movement, but for many others who reject or by-pass the church yet find in his teachings of love and compassion the key to a better world. They may or may not speak about the kingdom, but if Jesus is central, so ought also to be the basic note in his message.

A further reason for exploring this subject is to relieve the vacuity present in connection with the words spoken on innumerable occasions, "Thy kingdom come," and "thine is the kingdom, and the power, and the glory." The Lord's Prayer, in spite of the vogue of innovations, is still used almost universally in services of public worship. To many of us it is so familiar that we repeat it with our reflexes instead of with the mind and heart. But if challenged to say what this kingdom is for which we pray, many might be at a loss to give a reply.

It was mentioned above that many books on the kingdom of God have been written. This is true, but considerably more true of the first half of the twentieth century than of the period since that time. In the heyday of the liberal social gospel which occurred at the same time that form criticism and other important New Testament studies were making a fresh impact on Christian thought, the kingdom was considerably explored. Sometimes this was from the angle of the principles of Christian ethics believed to be derived from it, and again it centered on the attempt to explore the relations of apocalyptic to prophetic thought in the message of Jesus. As the social gospel came to be regarded as an aberration of liberal theology, discussion of the kingdom from this standpoint was interrupted. This demise was hastened by the rise of neo-orthodoxy, but has lasted beyond the neo-orthodox period into the present. The angle of New Testament criticism remained, but has taken a new turn toward the validity of the second coming and other aspects of a futuristic kingdom.

The watershed is to be found in the 1950s. Though no single event produced it, it came into focus in the ecumenical discussion of "Jesus Christ, the hope of the world," the main theme of the Evanston Assembly of the World Council of Churches in 1954. As three years of discussion by the preparatory commission on the main theme were summarized in successive releases, many Americans discovered to their surprise that the second coming of Christ, which they supposed had been relegated to the Pentecostals and other biblical literalists, was an active concern of eminent European theologians and the keynote in their understanding of the kingdom. Gradually, American thought became adjusted to the idea that when divested of its cruder settings, the return of Christ as the consummation of the kingdom needed to be taken seriously.

In recent years there has been a significant upturn of interest in the theology of hope. Two German theologians, Jürgen Moltmann and Wolfhart Pannenburg, have been most influential in this field. It has become prominent in American thinking as well, whether grounded in the Bible or in process theology. The theology of hope is of great importance and is related to the kingdom as a deduction from it. Yet it is not a substitute for an inclusive understanding of the kingdom. Furthermore, hope is not the only basic note in the meaning of the kingdom. This involves judgment as well as hope and calls for obedience and commitment in every aspect of Christian living.

From the standpoint of popular appeal, hope is a legitimate desire and is something that everybody needs and ought to be able to have. This is less acknowledged in current society in regard to other central aspects of the kingdom. Judgment is not a popular mood in today's world where the prevailing quest is for self-enjoyment, or at most for self-fulfillment, within congenial social relations. Obedience and commitment to the will of God are called for in "thy will be done on earth as it is in heaven." But such obedience and commitment are always costly with faith and love as the central requirements of the kingdom. Can these be judged as the dominant notes in today's world? Hardly.

We come then to the basic reason for the writing of this book. Most of the writings about the kingdom of late are of an academic nature, trying to discern from the biblical foundations a view which the author regards as the true one. This is important, and the present author will draw upon these studies to try to clarify and, in a measure, evaluate them. Our faith must rest upon true foundations as far as we can discern them. But this is not the main reason this project is undertaken. The reason lies in the spiritual hunger which is evident beneath the spiritual chaos and lack of compelling purpose in our time.

This spiritual hunger appears in many recent developments. We see it in the Jesus movement, the charismatic revival with its speaking in tongues, the growth in conservative churches while others decline in numbers and influence, the turn toward Eastern meditative cults, the upsurge once more of belief in an imminent second coming of Christ to put an end to the distresses of our time. All these moods and movements give hope and assurance to some people. What is lacking in them is a clear understanding of the life-giving personal and social relevance of the kingdom of God. This gives hope; it calls for repentance and offers renewal; it demands obedience to the will of God; it summons us to love one another. Nothing is more needed in our time or in any other.

Instead of waiting for somebody else to write the book that I believe is needed, I decided to undertake it. The first chapter will assess the dilemma we are in. Then, the second will be a rapid survey of the movement of thought in this matter in the twentieth century. I have lived through much of it either as an observer or participant, and this should lend some perspective. Four major types of kingdom theory are reviewed with an attempt at their evaluation.

Chapter 3 will present the author's own understanding of the kingdom of God. This might logically be deferred until after the grounds for holding it are presented, but it is placed here so that if the reader desires, he may compare it with the positions surveyed in the previous chapter.

The next two chapters present these grounds by way of following the injunction to search the Scriptures. Their aim is to examine as closely as possible what Jesus believed about the kingdom when he made it his central message. Chapter 4, entitled "The Kingdom Before and After Jesus," looks at the origins of this concept in the Old Testament and the intertestamental period and then at what was made of it in the early church. Chapter 5, "The Kingdom in the Parables," examines these as the primary source of our knowledge of the basic message of Jesus.

The last two chapters turn from theological analysis and biblical study to the relations of these to the individual Christian and to the message and the service of the churches in the present world. Hence, they deal with the difference a better understanding of the kingdom might make in strengthening hope and courage, overcoming divisive forms of polarization in the churches, and redirecting action toward greater human good. The final chapter sums up what the Christian may believe, not with precise knowledge but with reasonable assurance, about life after death and the future coming of the kingdom, with the relationship between these two grounds of hope.

The author makes no claim to have said the authoritative word in any of these disputed, but vitally important, issues. This is simply the outcome of one person's lifetime of thinking. But if the book moves Christians and their churches a step toward clarity, understanding, and effectiveness of action, it will have served its purpose.

UNDERSTANDING THE KINGDOM OF GOD

Where We Stand

Jesus preached the kingdom of God. We preach Jesus. In him and through the power of his message the kingdom is available to us. But can we preach Jesus or even understand him without understanding God's kingly rule, the central note in all his preaching?

1. The popularity of Jesus

In our time there has been a remarkable increase in the popularity of Jesus. This is not to deny that in one way or another he has always been central to Christianity. But today this centrality has taken on a new emphasis. About God there is considerable doubt and uncertainty, not only in the secular world but in Christian circles as well, with various attempts to preserve the meaning and value of God for human experience without the personal God of historic Christian faith. The churches, long the primary carrier of the gospel that centers in Jesus Christ, are the recipients of many attacks. Some of these are merited, while more are based on the misunderstandings accruing from noninvolvement. But central to these charges is the complaint that the churches have forsaken the teachings, the example, and the commands of Christianity's founder.

Occasionally we hear the oft-repeated charge of former days, that Jesus was an impractical dreamer. But not often. Not only is Jesus not under criticism by the press or the public, he is the center of important movements. A few years ago when the death-of-God theology was claiming much popular attention, its exponents advocated the substitution of loyalty to Jesus. This homage they were willing to render in full measure to him even while decrying the God whom Jesus worshiped and served, from whom he drew his message, its power, and the nature of his own living and dying.

Today the Jesus movement has enlisted the concern of thousands of modern youth, some of them within the churches, but more of them church dropouts or the products of nonreligious homes. Usually ultraconservative in theology, seriously limited in their awareness of what full discipleship would mean, certainly unschooled in the subtleties of New Testament scholarship, they nevertheless find in Jesus their Lord and Savior. And their lives are changed thereby! Such a commitment to Jesus amid the claims and counterclaims of a secular society needs to be understood rather than disparaged, and, if possible, directed toward a larger vision of Jesus and his message for the totality of human life.[1]

Personal conversion is not the only sphere in which Jesus lays claim to life today. It is one of the encouraging facts of our time that in the churches there is a growing sense of the need for Christians to be involved in political and other forms of social action. To be sure, this impulse is far from general, and there are many who want the churches to stick to "spiritual" matters, to "preach the gospel" instead of social change, and in particular, not to "meddle in politics." Yet, the recognition that the gospel relates to the whole of life is more common today, even in the conservative churches, than it has ever been. Many ministers discerned the vital need of social action in the time of the liberal social gospel in the earlier part of this century. But now under other names this movement is more widespread. It comes through various channels, but its source appears to be a more realistic awareness of the love commandment of Jesus.

This appears even in the most unconventional and revolutionary movements. Many young people are unconnected with either the Jesus movement or the churches; yet they find in Jesus their authority for anti-war, anti-injustice, anti-establishment, and other social protests.

Though we may rejoice that Jesus is in such good standing today, there are perils in this popularity. One of his own most significant sayings is, "Woe to you, when all men speak well of you, for so their fathers did to the false prophets" (Luke 6:26). There is no danger that we shall discover him to be a false prophet. Yet it is much easier to praise Jesus than to follow him. When he bids us to seek first the kingdom of God and his righteousness, it is a costly demand all too easily glossed over.

But of this, more later. Our concern now is to ask what there is about Jesus that leads so many to speak well of him.

2. The miracle of Jesus

The rise in the popularity of Jesus has reasons. To cite a familiar adage, when it is darkest we can see the stars. This is a dark time; men and women must have hope or perish in apathy and discouragement. And there is not much in the surrounding culture, with all its achievements and its glitter, to elicit hope. The shadows cast a few years ago by the threat of impending atomic destruction have lightened somewhat, only to be replaced in popular attention by an awareness of ecological danger and the energy crisis. War, poverty, violence, racial tension, and human exploitation continue to darken the scene. The vision of the American dream with its great ideals and dedication to the good of mankind has become clouded, not only by social and political disorder and revelations of immorality, but by the prevalence of a self-centered hedonism which finds expression in a feverish quest for enjoyment.

In such a sick society, the star of Jesus shines with a greater brilliance. Here, it seems to many, is one way of life, one source of inner power, one flame of hope, one call to an upward course, which without reservation can be depended on.

This is a true intuition. It is a spontaneous witness to the uniqueness of Jesus and the truth imbedded in his message that men cling to him, not only in good times, but when other supports prove undependable. It is the power of Jesus to speak to all sorts and conditions of men in all circumstances that has given Christianity its tenacity through the centuries. Some fifty years ago H. G. Wells, certainly an informed historian and keen analyst of human affairs, said of Jesus: "His is easily the dominant figure of history. . . . A historian without any theological bias whatever would find that he simply cannot portray the progress of humanity honestly without giving a foremost place to a penniless teacher from Nazareth." [2]

Whatever may be thought about the miracles of Jesus, he himself is the greatest miracle of all. For a peasant woman's child in occupied territory in an out-of-the-way corner of the Roman Empire to have become the man he did, attracting what looked like flash-in-the-pan attention during his brief years of ministry, unknown to most of his contemporaries and viewed as an upstart, a wonder-worker, or a fanatic by most of those who knew about him, dying a felon's death deserted by most of his close and trusted friends with the incredible rumor then circulated that he had risen again—what chance had he of any lasting fame? For such a man to occupy a foremost place in history, and to continue to occupy it after nineteen centuries and more, is unexplainable on any ordinary grounds.

What chance had this man of leaving anything behind him after he had tangled with the ruling powers for saying things which seemed to them treasonable or blasphemous, or both? Yet one cannot narrate the history of the Western world and leave

Jesus out. One cannot consider the great music or art or literature of the centuries and leave Jesus out. His words are imbedded in our language and, let us hope, in our consciences as well. It is an exaggeration to say that every advancement in the Western world has stemmed from him, but so much has that this in itself is a miracle. When we think of all that has come from him in the impulse toward human freedom and dignity—the challenge of ignorance and the attempt to remedy it, the concern for and conquest of disease, the sensitivity to the needs and plight of the weak, destitute, helpless, and those in every kind of suffering, the stabilizing of the inner lives of millions of his followers around the world, and the fostering of a prophetic attack on such giant social evils as prejudice, injustice, and war—when we consider the things that have stemmed from this "penniless teacher of Nazareth," we are dull indeed if the wonder of it does not sweep over our souls.

3. The problems emerge

The appeal of Jesus through the centuries to the many vital angles of human experience is such that we need not wonder when many people today give him high praise and a good press. We do well to rejoice in the lives committed to him, whatever the need of variations in the forms and enrichment in their expressions. That Jesus is still Lord and Savior marks him as the supreme disclosure of God and the authentic and unique Son of God. But because this is so, it is the more imperative that we look carefully at the many facets of his message.

There are problems that need to be confronted if one is to grasp the message of Jesus and build one's life upon it. Too often they are glossed over or only superficially understood. All of them are related to his central message, the kingdom of God. Hence, the writing of this book.

Some of these problems are practical, moral, and existential. In short, they have to do with the soul of the follower of Jesus—his personal faith, his moral decisions in the many crises of everyday life, his power for living, and his attitudes toward dying. We must sort out the perennial from the peripheral and socially-conditioned elements in the words attributed to Jesus in the record. There is a peril in modernizing Jesus[3] in view of the fact that he lived in a very remote, pre-industrial society nearly two thousand years ago. The conditions within which we must make decisions now are very different. This is often pointed out and needs to be. But there is also a peril in *not* modernizing Jesus to the point of seeing the relevance of his spirit and basic teachings to the life of today.

Again, there is the problem that Jesus left few specific directives for decision-making. How much easier it would be if we could turn to him and find a legal code to go by! But probably it is better that he did not leave many directives. The one most specific, his prohibition of divorce, turns out to cause a good deal of suffering when rigidly adhered to. And where would the economic foundations of society be if there were a large-scale, literal observance of the injunction, "Give to him who begs from you, and do not refuse him who would borrow from you"? (Matt. 5:42).

Another problem of a practical and spiritual nature arises from apparent inconsistencies, or at least profound paradoxes, that emerge when individual passages are cited. For example: "Come to me, all who labor and are heavy laden, and I will give you rest. For my yoke is easy, and my burden is light" (Matt. 11:28, 30). Many in deep trouble and anxiety have found rest for the soul in this promise, and it is one of the most precious assurances of our faith. But look a little further in the same Gospel, and we find Jesus saying: "If any man would come after me, let him deny himself and take up his cross and follow me. For whoever would save his life will lose it, and whoever loses his life for my sake will find it" (Matt. 16:24–25). Here are summarized the demands of the gospel. While Christian experience validates both statements, distortions arise from accepting one without the other. Much of today's adulation of Jesus is questionable in the light of his call to self-denial. For to seek for one's self a kind of euphoria, even if it is the spiritual euphoria of celebrating one's adoration of Jesus, is not to seek first the kingdom of God and his righteousness.

Look further at this last injunction, and another kind of problem emerges. "But seek first his kingdom and his righteousness, and all these things shall be yours as well" (Matt. 6:33). According to the context, "these things" are food, drink, and clothing, and can easily be extended to include shelter and other material necessities—money to pay the rent and to buy the groceries. But is this in accord with experienced realities? The evidence appears to be to the contrary. Christian fidelity may or may not be rewarded in this manner. Those denied the basic physical foundations of "the good life" are quite apt to be as good Christians and as saintly souls as those who are able to live in comfort. If they are not, the reason may often be found in the lack of these necessities which our Lord elsewhere bids us to share with those in need. There is no neat correlation between the kingdom of God and prospering in this world's goods; in fact, we are warned of the peril of riches to the soul.

A familiar problem in the interpretation of the words of Jesus—a problem which has evoked interminable discussion and is basic to the most serious of all social issues—is the attitude of Jesus toward violence and hence toward war. One may quote, "for all who take the sword will perish by the sword" (Matt. 26:52), only to find it immediately countered with, "Do not think that I have come to bring peace on earth; I have not come to bring peace, but a sword" (Matt. 10:34). In the Sermon on the Mount there is the familiar and often debated word, "Do not resist one who is evil. But if any one strikes you on the right cheek, turn to him the other also" (Matt. 5:39). This at least evokes debate. But there is a passage in Luke so cruel and vindictive in its implications, so unlike the whole spirit of Jesus, that it is seldom quoted, if indeed it is discovered. "But as for these enemies of mine, who did not want me to reign over them, bring them here and slay them before me" (Luke 19:27). Any but the most confirmed literalist will question whether Jesus ever said such a thing, even as the punch line of a parable.[4]

We are not left mute before such matters. These apparent inconsistencies in the words of Jesus can be at least partially explained by an understanding of how the New Testament was compiled and of the influences that played upon those early Christians who took the oral tradition and wrote it down as a connected narrative. There is also a basic polarity in the Christian message, with its great demands and equally great assurances, which accounts for the apparent disparity in some statements.

Yet after these factors have been taken into account, there still remain inconsistencies in the words of Jesus. These important, but relatively understandable, problems have been surveyed as preparation for a much more baffling one. This is found in what is most central to the message of Jesus—the nature of the kingdom of God. Imbedded in the question of its nature are the issues of when and where and how it is to come. A case can be made for its having come in the past with the coming of Jesus, for its gradual growth in the present, or for its coming only in the future with a catastrophic end of the earthly scene. Some believe that Jesus preached its coming on earth and taught us to labor and pray for it; while others place it either at the end of earthly history or totally beyond it in a transcendent realm. Some would make it solely a personal inner commitment, while others have identified its coming with a transformed society. Running throughout all these variants is the question of whether Christ's followers as the servants of God have a responsibility for bringing it to pass—"building the kingdom" is the phrase formerly often heard—or whether God in his wisdom and power will usher in the kingdom in his own good time.

There are enough differences of opinion on these points—and all of them defended from some statements in the New Testament—to keep us busy for the remainder of this book. But, first, let us outline the primary grounds of these differences.

4. Prophetic or apocalyptic?

There is a dual strain in the recorded words of Jesus in reference to the kingdom of God, and from this divergence stem most of the other variants listed above. Within each strain there is a reasonable degree of consistency; but this consistency disappears when one of them is set over against the other.

It is not difficult to summarize the understanding of the kingdom which is prevalent in most of the mainline churches. It seems clear enough that the kingdom of God means the rule of God over his world (especially over man, his supreme creation) and the assurance of God's presence and support that requires of us reciprocal obligations. It carries with it the call to obedience, both within the individual soul and in the total relationship of persons within the whole. Our supreme moral endeavor is to strive in manifold ways for the advancement of God's kingdom throughout the world. Thus, when we pray "Thy kingdom come," we call upon God to assist in our effort to bring the state of mankind into conformity with the divine will.

This understanding of the kingdom, though expressed in other language, is in conformity with not only a major thrust in the teaching of Jesus, but of the prophets as well. It is previsioned in

Jeremiah as a new covenant written in the hearts of men (Jer. 31:31–34). We see it foreshadowed in Second Isaiah's portrayal of the Suffering Servant as the true Messiah. It is coherent with the call of Jesus to the way of love as he states it in the two great commandments which lie at the base of our moral and spiritual obligation (Matt. 22:35–40; Mark 12:28–31; Luke 10:25–28). This note of God's rulership in conjunction with the requirements which this lays upon us is sounded again and again in the parables of the kingdom which make up a large part of the first three Gospels.

This interpretation of the kingdom of God, though it usually comes without a special name, may be designated as the prophetic conception of the kingdom. It views Jesus standing within the great succession of the Old Testament prophets; however, it does not limit him to that or deny his uniqueness as the supreme disclosure of God, the Son of God, and the Christ.

This general point of view has been stated in various ways, but I have not found it better expressed in terms of what it both does and does not imply than in the words of a distinguished New Testament scholar, Frederick Grant, in his book *The Gospel of the Kingdom.*

What I have tried to do is to see the movement of primitive Christianity as a whole and against its total background, political and economic as well as religious. . . . The result is a picture of Jesus as a prophet and a teacher—but one who was 'more than a prophet' and certainly one who taught 'not as the scribes'—rather than as a social reformer, the 'founder' of a religious movement, an ethical philosopher, or a fanatical apocalyptist. All these interpretations owe something to his teaching, seize upon and elaborate one or another element in its manifold variety; but none of them, nor all of them taken together, suffice to account for him. After all, Jesus was unique, and does not fit any specified category, ancient or modern. And his Gospel, though not a pattern of an ecclesiastical system nor yet a program for modern social reform, is still 'social' through and through—social *because* religious, in the ancient biblical understanding of religion.[5]

If this prophetic note in the words of Jesus were all we find in the records, we should still have the problem of discovering and doing the will of God as servants in his kingdom amid all the manifold complexities of our time. But it is not all.

Deeply imbedded in the records are both incidental sayings and extensive passages which point toward a catastrophic end of the earthly scene. A great transformation will suddenly take place in which the souls of the righteous will be separated from those of the ungodly, the latter will be condemned to eternal punishment, and Christ having come again will reign in glory with his saints. In some passages this second coming of Christ is presented as a visible descent through the clouds, comparable to the account in the first chapter of Acts of his ascension into heaven (Acts 1:6–11). Not only is "the Son of man coming on the clouds of heaven" (Matt. 24:30), but vivid accounts are given of the "wars and rumors of wars" when "nation will rise against nation, and kingdom against kingdom" and other forms of evil and turmoil will give warning that the end is near (Matt. 24:1–35; Mark 13:1–31; Luke 21:5–36). This cannot be dismissed as a passing reference, for all three of the Synoptic Gospels give an extended account of these woes and warnings after which the Son of man will come with power and great glory to gather his elect from the four winds, and the kingdom will come.

The book of Revelation contains much in a similar vein. We are told that Christ will reign on this earth for a thousand years, after which there will be a great last battle and victory at Armageddon. This millenial imagery in the twentieth chapter of Revelation is sufficiently ambiguous to cause the premillenialists of today to place the victory over Satan at the beginning of Christ's return and reign, while the postmillenialists hold that God's kingdom will come to its consummation and fulfillment at the end of this period.

27

This general position has various nuances but, taken as a whole, it is an apocalyptic view of the coming of the kingdom of God. The terms apocalypse and eschatology are often used interchangeably, but the latter is the more inclusive. Eschatology, from the Greek *eschaton* or "the end," is the doctrine of last things. It includes whatever may be believed about the ultimate future of the world or our own life after death. Heaven, hell, purgatory, resurrection, personal immortality, and final judgment are all eschatological concepts, as is the kingdom of God when it is viewed in the light of a final consummation. In short, when the common, often casual question, "What is the world coming to?" is taken seriously, this is an eschatological inquiry.

What is distinctive about apocalypse is its visionary nature, with signs and wonders and many predictions, often with very vivid imagery. It usually centers in the foretelling of events which it is believed will take place at a particular point in time, whether precisely predictable or somewhat hidden from our imperfect knowledge. Whatever comes to pass will have major dramatic accompaniments. There is apocalypse in the Old Testament, especially in the book of Daniel. It abounds in the intertestamental period and is, as we have noted, ascribed to Jesus in the New Testament.

Eschatology is the more general term for the expectation of a new order which will come to replace the present world. This becomes apocalyptic when the attempt is made to picture in advance the form the new world will take, the series of events that will accompany it, and the signs that indicate the nearness of its coming. A point of much importance in the apocalyptic passages attributed to Jesus is the imminence of the end. The woes will be experienced, false Christs and false prophets will arise, and then—in the near future—the cosmic drama will occur. Jesus bids his followers to be watchful and not expect to know the exact time, which is known only to the Father. Yet as surely as summer follows the appearance of leaves upon the fig tree, it is coming. "Truly, I say to you, this generation will not pass away till all these things take place" (Matt. 24:34). See also Mark 13:30 and Luke 21:32.

Whatever we may think about whether Jesus expected a speedy end of the world, the early church without question did expect it. But it did not happen. These apocalyptic expectations gradually subsided, only to rise again with full force just before the year 1000. But with the same result. Again and again the time of Christ's coming has been predicted, one of the most famous occasions being the Millerite movement of the 1840s, when many sold their property and donned white robes for the great event on the night of March 21, 1843. This group, sobered in expectations but undaunted, have since rendered great service through their hospitals as the Seventh-Day Adventists. The Millenial Dawn group expected Christ's return in 1914. They are now the Jehovah's Witnesses. Their periodical, *The Watchtower,* which was founded a hundred years ago by their famous pastor Charles T. Russell, is still being brought to your door by faithful witnesses.

We are now experiencing a revival of this expectation. To many, the state of the world seems to give clear evidence that these are the warnings of Christ's imminent return in judgment on the evil and in redemption of the righteous. Bumper stickers announce that Christ is coming soon, and a spate of books are being published which, whether read or not, are being sold in very great numbers. [6]

5. Our dilemma

While the mainline churches have, for the most part, long since ceased to expect a visible return of Christ, this expectation has never been given up in the more conservative groups. Furthermore, there are first-rank theologians and biblical scholars who, though they have rejected the crude literalism of a descent of Christ through the clouds as the mythological product of a prescientific age, nevertheless use the language of a second coming to designate the final consummation of the kingdom.

If this seems surprising, we have only to look at the prevalence of this concept in the New Testament. The *parousia* (from the Greek which means "to be near") as Christ's return is called in scholarly language, is promised again and again. In Matthew 24, Mark 13, and Luke 21, almost identical accounts are given. Mark's account is generally regarded as the original. While Matthew and Luke frequently draw from a common earlier source, Mark's account is often somewhat different. In Matthew 25 there is a strongly prophetic strain in the injunctions to compassion for and service to the needy, yet it is in the apocalyptic setting of a great last judgment. More incidental references are found in all four of the Gospels, in Acts, and in the letters, whether of Paul or other writers. An extensive list of these will be found in the notes.[7]

It is certain that the early church believed that Christ was coming soon. It is equally certain that this *parousia* did not occur, save as the living Christ as Holy Spirit indwelt his followers from Pentecost onward. What is not certain, and it has enlisted an endless amount of speculation, is what Jesus himself believed about it. New Testament scholars are virtually unanimous in their belief that the Gospels reflect the thinking of the early church in which these writings were compiled. There is no unanimity as to how much they embody the authentic words of Jesus.

From one angle, this finding of the biblical scholars, that we cannot say with certainty that we have the exact words of Jesus, relieves the dilemma. If Jesus expected his own dramatic return and a cataclysmic end of the world, and it did not happen, then he was in error at a crucial point in his message. The biblical writers were fallible persons like ourselves and could have made mistakes, the more probably because current Jewish thought was full of apocalyptic imagery. In the time gap between the ministry of Jesus and the earliest written records, it could have been attributed to him.

But can we assume this in faithfulness to the total record? And can we believe that Jesus made the kingdom the central note in his message, taught his followers to pray "thy kingdom come," with many poignant parables of the kingdom, and then had all this apocalyptic matter only grafted onto it? It looks very much interwoven with it.

So this is our dilemma. What kind of coming kingdom did Jesus expect? What did he believe about his own return? Is there an eschatology which can take into account both the biblical record and the deepest insights of our faith?

This must be our inquiry in the ensuing chapters. The next chapter will trace with rapid strokes the major attempts that have been made within the twentieth century to solve this problem. From this survey we may find some guidelines, not for a solution, but at least for a defensible opinion.

||
The
Spectrum of Opinion

The purpose of this chapter is to provide for the general reader a survey of the shifting nuances of opinion on the kingdom of God which have been held and seriously advanced by competent biblical scholars and theologians during the twentieth century. By no means can all of them be included. There are too many for that, and to multiply names would neither interest nor enlighten the reader. Nor can the arguments and citations of each writer be presented in minute detail. To do so would require a book devoted to nothing else, indeed, an entire shelf of books. What can be done is to state a dominant point of view with its main line of defense, and indicate something of the points at which it seems to be valid or vulnerable.

1. Apocalyptic eschatology

Around the turn of the century a position was developed by Johannes Weiss and Albrecht (better known as Albert) Schweitzer in Germany. It was mainly originated by Weiss but popularized by Schweitzer, and to it the latter gave the name of *consequente Eschatologie*. This is sometimes translated as "consistent eschatology" and again as "thoroughgoing eschatology." It is doubtful, as we shall note later, that it was either consistent or thoroughgoing, but the name has stuck.

Johannes Weiss (1863–1914) was the son of a noted New Testament scholar, Bernhard Weiss, and the son-in-law of a more noted theologian, Albrecht Ritschl. This relationship is of some importance, for Weiss developed a point of view that is steeped in New Testament textual and historical criticism but is more far out than that of his father and much at variance with the nineteenth-century liberalism of Ritschl. While Weiss attacked vigorously Ritschl's ethical and teleological understanding of the kingdom of God, he nevertheless was willing to grant that for Christian living in the modern world, this was the better point of view. He merits more attention than has usually been afforded him.

Weiss inaugurated this eschatological emphasis by publishing in 1892 a short work of sixty-seven pages entitled *Die Predigt Jesu vom Reiche Gottes,* recently republished in English after many years of oversight as *Jesus' Proclamation of the Kingdom of God.*[1] The book created such a storm of criticism as to lead him to bring out a considerably enlarged edition in 1900, which was virtually a new book with the same title. The main point of the position he advanced was that Jesus was not a modern man but a thoroughgoing apocalyptist, and therefore it is important not to read into his teachings ideas foreign to his world or to his thought. His attack on Ritschl, which was at the same time an attack on the whole trend of liberal theology at that time, was against the assumption that authentic lives of Jesus could be written which would portray him as a moral teacher urging men to build the kingdom of God by their labors.

At three points in particular Weiss attacked the prevalent liberalism. One was for its overlooking the antithesis between the kingdom of God and the kingdom of Satan. Not only was Satan to be cast down at the final crisis, but the exorcisms of Jesus were a sign of this coming event. A second basic error, he believed, was the assumption that Jesus, by his coming, ushered in a new era in the continuing development of the stream of history. Whereas, Jesus himself foresaw and taught the imminent end of the world and of history by an abrupt incursion of God into the human scene. A third error lay in putting the emphasis on human effort to bring about the kingdom, whereas God alone, by his kingly power, will bring it to pass when in his divine wisdom the season is right.

If these points should sound to the reader like neo-orthodox or Barthian protests against more recent forms of liberalism, there is a reason, for there is a direct line of succession. Some of these connections will become evident later in this chapter. It should be clear, however, that the biblical literalist can find no comfort in these affirmations, for they rest on grounds quite other than those of fundamentalism. They are based on extensive studies of the complex processes by which the New Testament was produced. These led to the belief that complete historical accuracy cannot be attributed to the words of Jesus, yet with the conclusion that the apocalyptic sayings ascribed to him give us, if not his exact words, a true picture of his point of view.

Weiss, with scholarly reserve, dealt only with the teachings of Jesus and did not attempt any reconstruction of his ministry or life story as it appears in the Gospels. His startling affirmation of an apocalytic kingdom of God in Jesus' outlook brought him critical attack from many and approval from some. A somewhat younger contemporary, who was destined to live much longer and have a more lasting influence, was much impressed by it. It was he who introduced this promise into the main stream of Christian thought. We must look now at the work of Albert Schweitzer (1875–1965), regretfully passing by his great work as an interpreter of Bach and as a medical doctor in the Congo to deal only with his contribution as a theologian.

Schweitzer's first published work to deal with this theme was *The Secret of Jesus' Messiahship and Passion,* now more commonly known as *The Mystery of the Kingdom of God,* which appeared in 1901.[2] However, his far more influential work appeared in 1906, *The Quest of the Historical Jesus,*[3] which is still read and quoted. Published originally with the title *From Reimarus to Wrede,* it could hardly have been expected to leave such an impact, for it is mainly a survey of biblical scholarship in regard to Jesus between the writings of Reimarus in 1778 and Wrede in 1901. Only toward the end of the book does Schweitzer give a full and direct statement of his own eschatological position. This proved to be arresting enough to make the book live. It has gone through numerous editions, and in title and partially in content it forms the backdrop of the new quest of the historical Jesus of which much is being heard today.[4]

While this book transmits rather than originates the apocalyptic position which Weiss had set forth, it popularized this position and created much more stir in the theological world. Seldom after that did a major biblical scholar attempt to write a life of Jesus, which had been commonly done in the previous century. Günther Bornkamm, fifty years after Schweitzer had proved its impossibility, was brave enough to produce such a book in 1956. In it he says of Schweitzer's work that it was at one and the same time a memorial to the liberal quest of the historical Jesus and its funeral oration.[5]

While Weiss had dealt only with the teachings of Jesus, Schweitzer extended the presentation to include what he believed could, and could not, be known with reasonable assurance about the life of Jesus. The result is the contention that the entire life, work, and teaching of Jesus was dominated by an eschatological expectation to be understood only in terms of Jewish apocalyptic assumptions and writings. Schweitzer theorizes that Jesus believed the end to be so imminent that he expected it to occur before the disciples' return from the mission reported in Matthew 10. Then when this did not take place he decided that his own messianic vocation was to die, for his death would bring about the coming of the kingdom and his manifestation as the expected Son of man.

The one human requirement for a place in the kingdom would be repentance. The ethical teachings were given to form the criterion of repentance and were to apply only to the brief period before its coming. Hence, the ''interim ethic'' for which Schweitzer is famous. The ethical implications of the Sermon on the Mount as well as those of the parables are included in this category.

Thus, the kingdom in Schweitzer's understanding of Jesus is to come in the very near future but is still not present. The prayer ''Thy kingdom come'' testifies to its futurity. It is present only as its coming may be discerned by the events which foreshadow it. In fact, in the statement by which Schweitzer comes nearest to hinting that Jesus discerned its presence, he uses the simile of the shadow: ''It is present only as a cloud may be said to be present which throws its shadow upon the earth; its nearness, that is to say, is recognized by the paralysis of the Kingdom of Satan. In the fact that Jesus casts out the demons, the Pharisees are bidden to recognise, according to Matt. XII. 25-28, that the Kingdom of God is already come upon them.'' [6]

Since to Schweitzer the message of Jesus is wholly eschatological, the kingdom could not be understood simply as an inward spiritual reality. But that did not preclude the presence of the living Christ in and to the Christian believer. His own estimate of the significance of Jesus for the modern world is not based upon an apocalyptic hope that was unfulfilled either in New Testament times or since, but in the fact that Jesus speaks to and calls men as followers to his service today. This is stated in moving words at the conclusion of *The Quest of the Historical Jesus,* quoted so often that they have become a classic.

He comes to us as One unknown, without a name, as of old, by the lake-side, He came to those men who knew Him not. He speaks to us the same word: "Follow thou me!" and sets us to the tasks which He has to fulfil for our time. He commands. And to those who obey Him, whether they be wise or simple, He will reveal Himself in the toils, the conflicts, the sufferings which they shall pass through in His fellowship, and, as an ineffable mystery, they shall learn in their own experience Who He is.[7]

What shall we say of "thoroughgoing eschatology" as a whole? First, it is bold enough to take seriously the apocalyptic passages in the world of and in the recorded words of Jesus and to see that he was, in a measure, situation conditioned. This is not to say that Schweitzer was right in taking these passages as the dominant note in the message of Jesus. Yet it is too easy a way out of the dilemma to dismiss them all as first century interpolations.

A second contribution lies in the fact that Schweitzer never renounced his allegiance to Jesus or his sense of the validity of the call of Jesus to the service of human need. Jesus was certainly wrong in his expectation of an imminent and cataclysmic end of the present world and coming of the kingdom, yet he still remains our Lord who calls us to be his followers.

A third contribution comes out more clearly in Schweitzer's other major work among the considerable number he wrote, *The Mysticism of Paul the Apostle*.[8] There he maintains that Paul's conception of the kingdom, though he expected an imminent end of the world, was far from other-worldly in its bearing on the Christian life. The kingdom is not a human achievement, nor is it wholly a matter of personal piety. It is God's kingly rule to become manifest in the human scene through divine irruption from beyond it, and we await with faith and hope its consummation. "To be a Christian means to be possessed and dominated by a hope of the Kingdom of God." [9]

These are no small contributions. Yet Schweitzer's apocalyptic interpretations of Jesus are open to challenge. Perhaps the shortcoming most commonly pointed out is that he did not take seriously enough in his analysis the ethical teachings of Jesus in relation to the message of the kingdom. Thus, the "interim ethic" has met with minor support, and I know of no one who takes it seriously today. It has been charged that he formulated his apocalyptic position at the beginning of his study and then without full objectivity shaped his textual conclusions around it by regarding as authentic the passages which corroborate it.[10] Be that as it may, both Weiss and Schweitzer in their eschatology so largely bypassed the prophetic notes for the apocalyptic in the message of Jesus as not to be fully consistent or thoroughgoing. Eschatology is a broader term than apocalypse.

So, though there are constructive values in this school of thought, it was bound to be countered by others. We turn now to a very different approach.

2. Prophetic eschatology

It is difficult to know what to call the point of view to be considered in this section, for there is no single term for it that is generally agreed upon. While it has had many exponents, especially in America, no one like Schweitzer has given it a distinctive and lasting name, and various nuances of thought are embraced within it.

Its basic feature is that the central message of Jesus lies in the love commandment—love of neighbor as well as love of God—and this calls his followers to earnest and unremitting effort for the increase of love with justice throughout all humanity. This has received various emphases. In 1917 Walter Rauschenbusch, an early and outstanding exponent of it, brought out *A Theology for the Social Gospel.*[11] The position it defends is often referred to, usually today with disparagement, as the social gospel kingdom, though it embraces much more than a transformation of the world by political and economic action. A major theologian in recent years who has defended such a moral and ethical kingdom as basic to the message of Jesus is L. Harold DeWolf in *A Theology of the Living Church*. He stresses its religious nature as well and calls it the immanental as contrasted with the apocalyptic interpretation.[12] George E. Ladd in *Jesus and the Kingdom* settles for calling its various nuances simply "noneschatological interpretation." [13] Norman Perrin in his *The Kingdom of God in the Teaching of Jesus* dismisses it as being not authentically biblical in a chapter entitled "The American View of Jesus as a Prophet." [14]

As I shall attempt to indicate, I believe that this understanding of the kingdom is thoroughly grounded in its roots, though not in all its fruits, in the message of Jesus as we find it in the Bible. "Prophetic" is the best term by which to compare this point of view with the apocalyptic. I have used it in the brief introduction given in the previous chapter. This does not mean that Jesus was a prophet only. He is universal man sent by God with a supreme mission and rightly viewed as Son of God, Lord, and Savior. My mind and heart respond to the words in Matthew 11:9: "Why then did you go out? To see a prophet? Yes, I tell you, and more than a prophet." To designate the social-ethical kingdom as prophetic is open to misunderstanding since to many a prophet means a foreteller or predicter, which is closer to the apocalyptic view. Yet in the more authentic sense of a prophet as one who speaks for God to declare his word and will, Jesus and his message of the kingdom stand clearly in the prophetic tradition.

Whatever it may be called, what are the dominant notes in this view of the kingdom? First, it rejects completely the idea of Jesus' coming again on the clouds of heaven and with a dramatic cataclysm putting an end to earthly society. It does not deny that Jesus may have thought that the end was coming soon. In modern forms it grants that through human sin and folly life may indeed end on this planet—a possibility that has become the more acute through the unleashing of nuclear energy and the advance of ecological destruction. Yet to this prophetic or "immanental" point of view the apocalyptic passages in the Bible are a blend of first century thinking with symbolic imagery. They have meaning if interpreted mythologically in the light of the situations within which they emerged, but are not to be taken as literal fact or precise prediction.

But to be nonapocalyptic is not sufficient, for a negative approach does not do justice to the great affirmatives of Jesus. What is affirmed is the rule of God, in love and justice, over his total created world and especially over humanity as his supreme creation. This kingly rule is not a kingdom in the sense of a particular realm that is ruled over; it is the kingship or sovereignty of God over all. In no part of the world and among no people is God's kingly reign fully accepted. Hence, the sin and evil in human society. Yet at no point does God surrender his sovereignty to the devil or to the blind indifference of meaningless forces. Despite the world's misery and the ever-present fact of human sin, God's providential care is over all, and God's design impels us to service in love.

Man's responsibility, therefore, is to further the acceptance of God's rule and the meeting of God's demands through the increase of love and justice upon the earth. The essential meaning of "Thy kingdom come" is for an increase in the doing of God's will on earth, and hence for a greater acceptance of God's sovereignty through the elimination of barriers to God's will. This requires of God's servants faithful obedience in love.

But coming when? This point of view takes seriously the injunctions of Jesus not to try to set a time for it. Yet it will be a growth process, present in some measure now but advancing slowly because of the recalcitrance of the human spirit. This position has often been tied in with the evolutionary process, but this note is tangential rather than central to it. The parable of the mustard seed and of the leaven suggest its biblical rootage. The Sermon on the Mount and the parables of the kingdom are its principal charter. The love commandments of Jesus and his concern for the weak and helpless impel us to political and economic action in our time, although it is generally admitted that what Jesus was talking about was not particular strategies, but the relation of persons to God and to one another in every human relationship.

The limits of space permit only a quick review of the thought of some of its major exponents, but this may throw light on the forms it has taken and its stages of development.

This type of interpretation starts with Schleiermacher, the father of modern liberal theology, in the early part of the nineteenth century. He viewed Christianity as a form of tele-ological and ethical monotheism, in contrast with those Eastern religions which view existence as a cycle of rebirths from which the individual seeks escape. The *telos,* or "goal," toward which Christianity strives is the kingdom of God. It is through Christ the redeemer that this forward movement takes place, and the kingdom is the corporate human consciousness of God, experi-enced in a fellowship of believers through the living influence of Christ.

Albrecht Ritschl, from whom we noted that Weiss took his divergence, and Adolf Harnack, another great liberal German theologian, agreed with Schleiermacher's general position but with an important distinction. Instead of the kingdom's being summed up in Christian redemption, they said that Christianity should be viewed as an ellipse with two foci: one, the redemp-tion of the individual from his guilt into a new freedom in Christ; the other being the kingdom of God. The kingdom, then, is the moral restructuring and teleological advancement of humanity through action inspired by love. In brief, Christ redeems, but the redeemed are to establish the kingdom.

This had the effect of giving greater precision to the meaning of the kingdom and encouraging greater moral vigor. But it had also the result of drawing too sharp a line between personal and social religion—something that Jesus never did. This has persisted to the present. Taken up in America, this view of the kingdom spurred Christians to an attack on social evils never before taken seriously. It also tended to accent human effort to the point where some exponents of the social gospel forgot to say that while God calls us to activity in love as his servants, it is still God's kingdom, and he establishes it.

Walter Rauschenbusch in his exposition and theological defense of the social gospel did not fall into this error. He believed that the impulse toward a better society was the fruit of Jesus' proclamation of a kingdom of love, divine in its origin, growth, and consummation, sustained by the Holy Spirit, made manifest and operative as the will of God is done in human society. In his thought there was none of the utopian thought or ''evolutionary optimism'' often attributed to liberal theology and the social gospel movement by its critics. Though there was the note of hope through faith in God and fidelity to the call of Christ, his chapter on ''The Kingdom of Evil'' is starkly realistic in its portrayal of both the internal and the social barriers to the good life. In fact, in my own long association with this movement, I have never encountered anybody who doubted the power of evil in the world or who believed in automatic progress.

The chief defect in the thought of Rauschenbusch was that he did not take seriously enough the extensive apocalyptic passages in the Bible. This was true in general of the social gospel movement of the first half of the century, with the idea of a second coming or last judgment relegated to the Pentecostal sects. The social gospel itself was an enormously creative emphasis, and, while it declined in influence as neo-orthodoxy arose to challenge its liberal theological foundations, it survives to the present, mainly under other names.

After Rauschenbusch others wrote and many ministers preached the social imperatives of the kingdom. So commonly was this done that European theologians fell into the habit of referring to us as "American activists." The requirements of space prevent more than a brief look at two other authors in this succession.

Frederick C. Grant in 1940 wrote *The Gospel of the Kingdom* in which he disclaims completely the apocalyptic view, going so far as to say that it was too fantastic for a sane man like Jesus to have held.[15] His exposition of the prophetic element in the message of Jesus is unexcelled. He defends the social gospel but grounds it in the total religious outlook of Jesus, not in ethical imperatives only. The teaching of Jesus is not to be taken as a pattern for modern social reform, yet it is social through and through because it is religious in the deepest and fullest sense. It is a mistake "to represent Jesus as either a social reformer, an ethical philosopher, the founder of an institution, or an apocalyptic enthusiast." [16]

L. Harold DeWolf in his discussion of the meaning of the kingdom in *A Theology of the Living Church,* a textbook in systematic theology produced in 1953, deals little with the social gospel but holds that the apocalyptic and "immanental" strains in the Gospels are radically inconsistent.[17] After giving a carefully balanced statement of the biblical evidence for both views, he concludes that the apocalyptic is the result of bias in the oral reporting of the teaching of Jesus, which led to the substituting of a spectacular for a spiritual understanding of the kingdom. This was probably intensified by a misunderstanding of Jesus' predictions of national disaster.

Such solutions would present a welcome resolution of the

dilemma were it not for the fact that they presuppose a continuing world order, which Jesus apparently did not expect. The apocalyptic passages are too deeply imbedded in the Gospels for most biblical scholars to feel that they can be thus disposed of. So, we must turn now to another influential presentation.

3. Realized eschatology

The interpretation of the teaching of Jesus about the kingdom, which bears the name of realized eschatology, is always associated with the name of the distinguished British New Testament scholar, C. H. Dodd. This is not to say that in all its elements it is new, or that after nineteen centuries he discovered something in the New Testament that others had not found there. Yet, in *The Parables of the Kingdom* originally published in 1935 and in several later works he has proposed a view which is original enough to elicit a new name, and to command the respect of even those scholars who do not accept it.[18]

The principal note in realized eschatology is the contention that Jesus thought of the kingdom as having already come, an attainment brought into being through his coming as the Messiah and thus through his own ministry. The kingdom then is a present fact, not something to anticipate in the near or distant future. Eschatology in this sense does not have to do with the last things in a temporal sense but with ultimacy—with finality, not at the end of time and history, but with what is most real and most vital at all times in human existence.

The kingdom, therefore, is not to be viewed either as an apocalyptic breakthrough from another world to put an end to this one or as the goal of a long-continued social process within earthly history. The kingdom is here now because Christ has come to proclaim the gospel of judgment and salvation—though this is not to say that all have entered it. It was here in the person of Jesus and his ministry; it is here as the living Christ still speaks and transforms lives. The kingdom is the eternally present realm of God. It is eternity breaking into time in the presence of Jesus in his ministry, and after his death and resurrection in the presence of the Spirit within the church. The latter is the true *parousia*. The source of the kingdom is transcendent; it is the kingdom of *God*. Yet its presence is felt within this world, here and now, through the living Christ.

Dodd does not question Jesus' use of apocalyptic language. But he explains it by saying that Jesus used apocalyptic imagery "as a series of symbols standing for realities which the human mind cannot directly apprehend, and as such capable of various interpretation and re-interpretation as the lessons of history or a deepening understanding of the ways of God demand." [19] Such concepts, familiar to his hearers, as the awful fate of the unrighteous, the bliss of the redeemed, and the expected dramatic coming of the Son of man, were employed by Jesus to drive home to his hearers the ultimate and absolute nature of the kingdom and its entrance into history through the message which God had given him to proclaim.

While the apocalyptic passages, Dodd believes, can thus be accounted for, they do not provide the central ground for belief in realized eschatology. This is to be found in words of Jesus that are far less controversial. There are such basic passages as the initial summons of Jesus. "The time is fulfilled, and the kingdom of God is at hand; repent, and believe in the gospel" (Mark 1:15). Whether Luke 17:21 is rendered as in the King James Version (cited hereafter KJV), "The kingdom of God is within you," or more accurately as "in the midst of you," the time-setting is clearly in the present. An important passage is, "But if it is by the Spirit of God that I cast out demons, then the kingdom of God has come upon you" (Matt. 12:28). A cognate form in Luke 11:20 has a striking variation, "But if it is by the finger of God.'' In the charge of Jesus to the seventy as he sends them out on their mission, he bids them heal the sick and say to them, ''The kingdom of God has come near to you'' (Luke 10:9). A sharp break between the past and the present new order of the kingdom is suggested in Luke 16:16, ''The law and the prophets were until John; since then the good news of the kingdom of God is preached, and every one enters it violently.'' The final adverb is puzzling, but it probably suggests that there is no easy entrance into the kingdom in spite of its availability.

Professor Dodd points out that passages such as these have no parallel in Jewish teaching or the prayers then in use. This fact points to their being not only distinctive but the authentic words of Jesus.[20] However, it is in the parables that he finds the fullest evidence that Jesus believed he had been sent by God to inaugurate the kingdom. They present a crisis of decision and judgment that is not future but present. They set forth the new ethical requirements for entrance into and life in the kingdom. They embody the heart of the message of Jesus about the kingdom. ''Hence there is a place for ethical teaching, not as 'interim ethics,' but as a moral ideal for men who have 'accepted the Kingdom of God,' and live their lives in the presence of his judgment and His grace, now decisively revealed.'' [21]

Realized eschatology has been taken seriously. It has had the effect of bringing contemporary theology in general to the recognition that the kingdom of God must be in some sense present, however much it may be regarded as future also. It has much to commend it, for it reinterprets the apocalyptic passages without rejecting them, and it accents the present saving work of Christ. It makes a place for the moral imperatives of life in the kingdom. Still the problems persist. There are other passages, not simply those with striking apocalyptic imagery, but those in a more sober vein such as Mark 9:1 and Mark 13:30 which point clearly towards the future. And for the kingdom to be near or at hand, does that mean present or future? There is still room for difference of opinion.

4. The kingdom as existential decision[22]

We come now to one of the outstanding biblical scholars and theologians of the century, Rudolf Bultmann. Perhaps no one except Karl Barth has had a greater influence on Christian thought in our time, not only in person but through the students who have been his disciples but have modified his thought.

As foundation for understanding him we must reckon with the fact that for the past fifty years there has been an increasing amount of form criticism. This is the attempt to get behind the biblical records to their sources in oral tradition and written fragments, and thus to determine how individual passages, called pericopes, are related to each other. From this study in the New Testament, estimates are made as to what was probably the original form, and, therefore, how much in the Gospels can be taken as the authentic words and deeds of Jesus. We have encountered this before, but it becomes especially important to Bultmann's thought about Jesus and the kingdom.

As has been indicated, the biblical scholars as a result of their studies still differ not only as to the interpretation but the accuracy of the records of the sayings of Jesus. Bultmann goes further than most at this point and questions also the authenticity of the accounts of the ministry of Jesus, with the result that we know little about him. He says, furthermore, that it is not essential that we know what he did or what kind of man he was. He does not deny that Jesus lived and proclaimed a message which led to the founding of Christianity. Yet what is important is the effect of the message on the early church and, through this impact, the effect on the life experiences of people to the present. Thus, our understanding of Jesus must be existential.

But what of the apocalyptic passages? Here Bultmann follows in general the thought of Weiss and Schweitzer in their futuristic eschatology. But with a difference. They held these to be mainly the authentic words of Jesus, who predicted an imminent cataclysm and an end of the world which did not occur. Bultmann's view is that these, along with many other passages in the Bible which are the product of a prescientific age with thought patterns very different from ours, must be "demythologized." That is, we must stop trying to take them as they stand, but instead must try to see what the writers were getting at that is of permanent meaning. This does not, of course, mean that we should try to make an allegory of the passage or drag out of it a moral that was never intended. What needs to be done for any disputed passage of importance is to try to find its perennial meaning—that is to say, its existential meaning as it bears on the conditions of human existence and our lives today.

Bultmann finds the most important thing about the apocalyptic passages to be their stress on the *imminence* of the coming of the kingdom, and thus the urgency for human decision. This imminence is not temporal, but it is the nearness of God. We know, or at least can deduce, that Jesus repudiated the popular expectation of a messiah who would restore Israel to its former political greatness under King David, and that he substituted a spiritual call to repent, for the kingdom of heaven is at hand (Matt. 4:17; Mark 1:15). Thus, the kingdom is not already present in this call, but it is near, and this precipitates a crisis of personal decision as to whether one will accept for his life the reign of God.

Not only was this call issued in the first century, but it is a life and death decision with which God confronts every man. Each one of us stands, whether we recognize it or not, at a point of critical decision in our personal lives. God is the great demander who, from a realm beyond history, requires of us the decision to respond to his call within our human experience. This demand requires not only personal decision but moral obedience, not to merit a place in the kingdom by our goodness but to find it as the fruit of the new life. Jesus' ethics are set forth as the conditions of entrance into the coming kingdom, but in reality there is only one condition—complete obedience to the will of God.[23] Both the radical ethical teachings of Jesus and his proclamation of the kingdom find their unity in the crisis of decision before God.

Thus, the kingdom is available to all, but only at great personal cost. It is not the mistaken vision of Jesus about a coming world cataclysm and his return through the clouds of heaven. It is not a process of gradual growth in a continuing world order during which human effort brings it to pass. It is not something already present because of having been inaugurated by Jesus in his own person as the Messiah.[24] It is the supernatural, superhistorical gift of God to him who responds affirmatively to God in the ultimate—even eschatological decision of his own existence.

What shall we do with this interpretation? Have we at last found the key to this whole baffling matter? It relieves us of the necessity of trying to explain how Jesus could have been mistaken on so important a matter, and the demythologizing covers the entire gamut of miracle stories and a good many other puzzling passages. This is congenial to the mood of the Christian liberal who is fed up with fundamentalist literalism. On the other hand, it puts the emphasis at the point where the conservatives have always thought it to be central—on personal decision and surrender. In more erudite language it resembles the old familiar call to conversion, "Are you saved?"

Can these two moods be combined? Perhaps, but I doubt that Bultmann has done it. His picture of the Jesus of history is unnecessarily hypothetical and too tenuous to give an adequate foundation for the Christ of faith. The rallying cry of the early church in their witnessing and frequent martyrdoms was not to some dimly known figure who might have been somebody else. It was to Jesus Christ, the Son of God, the Savior, who had lived among men with a message and mode of life never seen or heard before. One who had given himself for their redemption, had been crucified, dead and buried, and had risen again to be with his followers as living Spirit through time and eternity.

So it is today under vastly changed external conditions. "What will you do with Christ?" is the ultimate, eschatological question. It relates deeply to how one orders his life and how he confronts his inevitable death. In short, it is the life-and-death matter that Bultmann says it is. This is why the meaning of the kingdom is far more than an academic question. But Bultmann's solution does not give us the full answer.

Does *any* solution give the answer? The ordinary Christian who has prayed all his life for the coming of the kingdom when he said the Lord's Prayer, and who thought he was being called to labor diligently for its advancement may be more confused than edified if he has read thus far in the book. Why all these complicated theories? And if the scholars cannot settle on what the kingdom is, or on when or how it is coming, or what Jesus really taught about it, why should I bother to try? That would be a natural response to this author's attempt to show that the problem is not as simple as it appears and the attempt to outline some of the principal types of approach to a solution.

There are points of truth and value in each of the four types of eschatology considered in this chapter. The apocalyptic stresses a sense of urgency and of God's power; the prophetic calls us to be active participants in the kingdom process; the realized type reminds us of the kingdom's immediacy; the call to existential decision again emphasizes urgency but without biblical literalism. There is truth in each of these thrusts if they can be amalgamated.

The Spectrum of Opinion

The author of this book is not presumptuous enough to suppose that she has the perfect solution. Yet she has an opinion on these matters which satisfies her mind and heart as adequate for Christian faith and life. Hence, she owes it to her readers to try to state it. This will be attempted in the next chapter.

III
What Is
the Kingdom of God?

At the end of the previous chapter the reader was promised a statement of what the author believes about the nature of the kingdom of God. There are two ways to arrive at such a position. One of them is through form criticism—a textual and literary analysis of the sources of the relevant biblical passages. This procedure over the past fifty years and more has rendered great service in a better understanding of the New Testament. Yet at the crucial point of Jesus' own understanding of the kingdom, there is still no agreement among competent scholars. Each of the positions previously outlined has plausibility if one attaches primary importance to one set of factors and gives little or no emphasis to others. This is evident from the fact that we have found values and shortcomings in each of the views of the kingdom which have been examined.

The other approach is to formulate, in as inclusive a manner as possible, a composite impression. This must be tested to see if it has adequate foundations. Such testing will require careful examination, not only of the known facts which support or oppose it, but of the intuitive, emotional, and rational considerations which have shaped this composite impression. Without claiming a completely scientific detachment, one forms a hypothesis and then proceeds to verify it. This verification is both by the objective historical and literary evidence and by the "reasons of the heart" which form so large a part of human existence and of Christian faith and experience in particular.

This is the type of procedure we shall now attempt to follow. Of course, it has its dangers. We noted that one of the criticisms directed against Schweitzer was that he formulated his position at the beginning of his studies and then regarded as authentic only the biblical passages which supported it. But this is not limited to Schweitzer. To a degree, all scholars do this because complete objectivity in any judgment is impossible. Yet if one knows that he is doing it and knows why he does it, the dangers of arbitrary choice based on wishful thinking or one's personal point of view may be somewhat eliminated.

1. A composite view

Such a composite understanding of the kingdom of God needs to be viewed on two levels. First, there are elements in it which are commonly recognized, though perhaps too seldom made specific, and on which there is little disagreement. Thus far we have dealt mainly with differences of opinion in order to make clear the dilemmas about its nature and forestall an oversimplification. Yet this should not obscure the fact that there are things to say about the kingdom which Christians who have given it any serious thought would seldom dispute. To be sure, these shade off quickly into differences of interpretation and application. Yet it is important and basic that there are some points of general agreement, for they form the foundation on which the other more diversified structures of opinion are erected.

In stating the composite view that this author regards as the most tenable, I will begin with convictions rooted in these general agreements. From that point it will be necessary to deal with the more disputed matters, and I shall then attempt to state where I stand on them and the reasons why.

First, the kingdom means the sovereign, righteous rule of God. It is a rule in which power and goodness, judgment and mercy are combined. Though the term arose when the nations were monarchies, and it had a more realistic symbolism then than now, it connotes power exercised, not in arbitrary dictatorial authority, but in loving concern. Jesus' understanding of God was of one whose power is supreme over all he has created, but whose love for every person is that of a father.

Second, this sovereign rule of God must be accepted by us in faithful, grateful obedience. There is no real kingdom without subjects. The kingdom is not destroyed by men's disobedience, for God still rules in judgment. Yet the summons to seek first his kingdom and his righteousness certainly entails human obedience. Without it, apathy breeds anarchy as the will of God is flouted.

Third, the goal of the kingdom is directed toward a redeemed society of persons. A redeemed society in this sense is not identical with a reconstructed social order, though this may well be one of the demands of seeking God's kingdom and his righteousness in obedience to the love commandments. A redeemed society is one in which salvation is sought and found, not as one individual alone, but in an over-expanding community of individuals. This is basic to the relation of the kingdom to the church, but the goal extends far beyond the boundaries of the visible church.

Fourth, the kingdom meets opposition at every point, and this opposition is latent even in our most meritorious actions. In short, no consideration of the kingdom should minimize the power of evil. The opposition may be thought of as coming from the devil, or from the demonic powers of history, or from mankind's ever-present sin, ignorance, apathy, and error. The "principalities and powers" confront God's power. God is never conquered by these forces, but what we believe to be his purposes are delayed or frustrated by them.

Fifth, the kingdom as God's rule is present but points forward. "Thy kingdom come." Though we may detect the evidences of its presence now, its consummation lies in the future. Whether this future is conceived as eternal life for the individual, or a new heaven and a new earth for mankind, or as the conquest of evil in or beyond human history, the trajectory is toward the future, the *eschaton*. A view of the kingdom of God need not be apocalyptic, but it is always in some sense eschatological.

To sum up, the kingdom of God is our ultimate challenge and our ultimate hope. Thus, it is not surprising that Jesus found in it his central message. It remains for us to discover, to declare, and to live by all that is good and true in what the term implies.[1]

Further convictions, more controversial, which I have arrived at in my own thinking may now be stated. I do not write as an advanced biblical scholar, but as one who has wrestled with the theological aspects of the question over a considerable span of years, and these are my conclusions.

In the thought of Jesus, there was a blend of the prophetic and apocalyptic elements inherited from his Jewish culture. He stood at the juncture of traditions from a long past, and as a thoughtful and concerned man of his times he could hardly fail to be familiar with and influenced by them. This is not to deny his uniqueness, of which I shall say more later. But we shall not get anywhere in trying to understand Jesus unless we are willing to see him as a man who stood within the course of history. This is the more crucial because any adequate understanding of the incarnation, which is basic to Christian faith, regards Jesus as both divine and human. Docetism, the denial of the humanity of Jesus on the claim that he only appeared to be human, was the first heresy with which the early church had to grapple, and it persistently lifts its head even today. Yet if Jesus were God and not man at all, there was no ground for the author of the fourth Gospel to say, "And the Word became flesh and dwelt among us, full of grace and truth'' (John 1:14), or for the church to build its faith upon this foundation throughout the centuries.

What we believe about the Jesus of history—about whom the Gospels tell much, though we wish we knew even more—will give the setting not only for the Christ of faith, but for a judgment about his central message of the kingdom. Whatever more Jesus was as God's Son and chosen agent of redemption and revelation, he was subject not only to historical and cultural influences but to elements of human finitude.

I believe that the prophetic and apocalyptic influences from the Hebrew scriptures and his inherited and surrounding culture were never fully amalgamated in the thought of Jesus. He probably felt no need, as our scholarly studies must, to sort out each strain and neatly balance them against each other. He did not try to keep them in separate categories or, on the other hand, to blend them with no rough places showing. There was wisdom from his fathers in all of the sacred writings! In short, Jesus did not feel it to be his vocation to engage in textual criticism or to be a systematic theologian, however important these enterprises may be as we study him.

Both the prophetic and the apocalyptic elements were absorbed into the mind and heart of Jesus. He also had a deep respect for the law which had had such a central place in the thought of his Jewish fathers. It was no casual word when he said, ''Think not that I have come to abolish the law and the prophets; I have come not to abolish them but to fulfill them'' (Matt. 5:17). What he desired with all his being was that all these inherited notes should be put on a deep, personal, God-centered basis.

So, in Jesus prophecy, apocalypse and law were transformed by the illuminating and overwhelming sense of God's utter sovereignty and his own call as God's servant to proclaim both the judgment and the saving love of God. What mattered to

Jesus was his mission to speak to men in their sin and call them to repentance, to set before them the mercy and goodness of God, to heal men's sickness of body and soul through the power of God, to call all who would listen to love God supremely and their fellow men as their own selves.

This message Jesus put in the familiar framework of the kingdom of God. He did not try to define the nature of the kingdom. What he did was to declare the urgency and hope of the kingdom, and set forth vividly in memorable affirmations and parables the conditions of entrance into it and the obligations of obedience within it. With such deep convictions gripping his soul, so all-important to him that he was ready to die for them, it is unlikely that he ever thought much about logical consistency. To demand this of him is to try to make of him something that he never felt to be his calling.

Both the prophetic and the apocalyptic notes were mingled in Jesus' messages of the kingdom, not as a simple carry-over from the past, but with a God-centered and love-and-justice-centered note which his own unique sense of relationship to God put into them. If we look at the composite whole of Jesus' message and ministry as those who loved him told and retold it until it came to be written in the form we have, the prophetic element predominates over the apocalyptic; yet it does not eliminate it. The more fantasic embellishments and harrowing threats connected with the last days can be attributed to imperfect reporting, not so much on the basis of textual criticism in which consensus is still lacking, but because they do not sound like Jesus. I do not go so far as to say with Frederick Grant that no sane man could have said them,[2] but I believe Jesus lived too close to God and knew too well the love of the Father for all his human children to have said them. Yet we do not need to reject all the apocalyptic passages, or deny that Jesus expected a speedy end of the world which did not occur. What Jesus thought of his own relation to

57

the long-expected Messiah is a question to which there is no clear and unambiguous answer. But from the frequency with which he calls himself the Son of man, he may have used this term, not solely as referring to his own humanity, as at some points seems its natural interpretation, but with the apocalyptic connotation it has in Daniel 7:13–14 and in the intertestamental Book of Enoch.[3]

Does it shatter our faith in Jesus to think that he may have been mistaken as to the imminent end of the world and the events that would surround it? Why should it? Doubtless those scholars are on safe ground who tell us that some of these passages were probably originally spoken by Jesus as predictions of his own death and resurrection. But even without this explanation, do we need to attribute to him omniscience and complete foreknowledge of the future? He probably did not know that the Western Hemisphere existed. He could not foresee what was going to be happening in the twentieth century. From Luke 19:41–44 we gather that he did expect destruction to fall upon his people because they knew not "the things that make for peace," but there is no likelihood that he knew just when or how this would happen as it did in A.D. 70. There is no indication that he foresaw the world's chronology being dated twenty centuries later from the supposed year of his birth.

We fall into docetism if we doubt that Jesus had human limitations. We know that he became weary and hungry and upon occasion experienced anger or grief. Then why doubt that there were some things about the future that he took over from the expectations rife in his time rather than from divine foreknowledge? In fact, in the apocalypse in Mark 13, he both declares the imminence of the consummation and his own ignorance of its exact time. "Truly, I say to you, this generation will not pass away before all these things take place" (Mark 13:30). Yet in a following verse he says, "But of that day or that hour no one knows, not even the angels in heaven, nor the Son, but only the Father'' (Mark 13:32).

It is for such considerations as these that I find no serious problem in discovering both prophetic and apocalyptic passages in the words of the Gospels attributed to Jesus. I do not believe that we have an exact record of what he did or said. Form criticism and the extensive biblical studies of the twentieth century have demonstrated that the Gospels are books of witness to the good news of Christ rather than exact and infallible historical accounts. Yet the portrait of Jesus still shines through them, sufficient for our Christian faith and life. The more we live with the light of the world which is the reason for the Gospels, the more clearly we are able to glean from them the urgency and hope of the message of the kingdom of God.

So, though I believe that the primary note in Jesus' understanding of the kingdom was the rule of God with a moral and spiritual message of the judgment, yet the loving kindness of God and of God's call to faithful obedience in all things, I do not believe that this prophetic note makes it necessary to reject wholly the apocalyptic. While Jesus seems to have accepted its particular terminology and some of its concepts familiar in his day, his apocalypticism is different. As in everything else, he gave illumination and fresh meaning to whatever he dealt with. His vision of the future is never in the mood of pessimism. It does not court the spectacular. Evil is not in command of creation. His call to trustful waiting and watchfulness suggests no renunciation of human effort. His apocalypticism is suffused with the spirit of God and given a moral character, as was everything he touched. The Son of man shall come in his glory—all the angels with him—and will sit on his glorious throne with all the nations gathered before him. Then the King will say to some, "Come, O blessed of my Father, inherit the kingdom prepared for you from the foundation of the world"

(Matt. 25:34). But it is the righteous who will hear this word, and the determining factor in the judgment is what men have done to their hungry, thirsty, naked, sick, imprisoned brothers. The King's great word is not a magisterial edict but a word that gives the true basis of kinship, "Truly, I say to you, as you did it to one of the least of these my brethren, you did it to me" (Matt. 25:40. See also 25:31–46). In this great parable of the last judgment there is a striking combination of apocalyptic thought with the prophetic. The keynote of the ministry and message of Jesus is summed up in another great passage, this time from his beloved Isaiah which he selected to read in the synagogue on the inaugural day of his ministry:

The Spirit of the Lord is upon me,
because he has anointed me to preach good news to the poor.
He has sent me to proclaim release to the captives
and recovering of sight to the blind,
to set at liberty those who are oppressed,
to proclaim the acceptable year of the Lord.
(Luke 4:18–19. Isa. 61:1–2).

Putting these considerations together, we find in the message of Jesus the foundations of what was outlined more formally at the beginning of this section as the essential notes about which there is large agreement among Christians. The kingdom means the righteous rule of God—a rule in which God is both King and Father. Therefore it is one in which God is above and beyond us in utter holiness, yet he is with us and within us in never-failing love. A philosopher might have something to say about the transcendence and the immanence of God, but Jesus was not concerned with philosophical terminology. The kingdom is both present with us, and it is coming. Yet it comes not by observation, and no man knows the hour of its coming. It comes gradually, like a mustard seed's growth into a mighty tree. It comes suddenly like a thief in the night and is to be anticipated with watchfulness, like a long-expected bridal procession. The kingdom is no solitary matter—it comes in a community which is the family of God. Its coming is a task set before us, to be prayed for, to be worked for, to be sought with the eagerness with which one sells all that he has in order to buy a treasure hidden in a field or a pearl of great price. Jesus did not say that it is our job to build the kingdom. Rather, it is our part to be the good ground in which the seed of the Sower can grow and bring forth much fruit.

Paradoxes? Yes, but not inconsistencies, unless we try to make of Jesus the strict logician that he never essayed to be. They are demonstrated in Christian experience as compatible. In his day the common people heard him gladly because he demonstrated in himself the reality of the kingdom by the warmth of his sympathy and the depth of his insight. In a blend of fidelity to Jesus as the Christ and to the kingdom which was his central message, the church has been able to find both a challenge to action and its ultimate hope.

Conference reports, adopted after much effort to say what all can agree to and hence subject to being considerably watered down, are often rather dull reading. One of the great experiences of my life was being a delegate to the Madras Conference of the International Missionary Council in 1938 and serving on two of its committees for drafting reports. The matter of the nature of the kingdom was then a very live issue, much more so than in recent years. By God's grace, it was with a solemn sense of having reached agreement where it seemed impossible that the committee finally came up with the following statement, and I quote it because I have not since seen a better one. I recall that it was E. Stanley Jones who gave it its final form.

The Kingdom of God is both present and future; both a growth and a final consummation by God. It is our task and our hope—our task which we face with the power of Christ; our hope that the last word will be spoken by God and that that last word will be victory. The Kingdom means both acceptance and action, a gift and a task. We work for it and we wait for it.[4]

2. Some differentiations of meaning

In the brief statement just quoted, and in most situations where the term the kingdom of God is under consideration, it is used in a number of different senses. These are related but not identical, and the amalgamation is usually made without consciousness of the difference. Such a distinction may or may not be needed, depending on the context. But before going further we had better attempt it. The five points listed earlier in the chapter may now be stated as three.

In the first sense, the kingdom of God means the eternal, ultimate sovereignty of God. In this sense *kingship* would be a more accurate term. This presupposes that God is not only the creator but the ruler of all he has made, and he remains so in spite of any thwarting of his will. As one of our familiar hymns puts it:

> This is my Father's world,
> O let me ne'er forget
> That though the wrong seems oft so strong,
> God is the ruler yet.

When we conclude the Lord's Prayer with the words, "For thine is the kingdom, and the power, and the glory," we affirm this divine kingship and our trust in God's ultimate authority and sovereignty.

A second meaning of the term is the rule of God among men insofar as this sovereignty is accepted and God's will is done. Although God is eternally king of the universe, including that very important part of it which is humanity, he has given us the freedom to reject this authority and follow our own disobedient desires. The kingdom is present wherever God's will is accepted and obeyed, and we may enter the kingdom wherever we are by giving him our loyalty. Since this is far from universal, we pray, "Thy kingdom come; thy will be done on earth."

A third meaning of the kingdom is the complete and final establishment of God's rule in the age to come, a final consummation in which God's will is fully done. This could come about by a long process of change, a gradual movement toward a fuller personal loyalty and a more Christian society on earth. The more common biblical understanding of it, however, is of a day of the Lord and a final judgment whereby only the righteous will receive a place in God's eternal kingdom, though there are hints also of an ultimate cosmic redemption through Christ.[5]

To sum up the relation of each of these concepts to human history, the first places the kingdom of God above history; the second within it; the third at the end, or beyond the end, of history. In regard to our own relation to it, there are corresponding differences. In the first sense, we are called to *acknowledge* the ultimate sovereignty of God. The kingdom, then, is God's gift to be gratefully accepted; it is the ground of our Christian faith and life. In the second sense, the kingdom is a present fact and we *participate in it* as we give our allegiance to God and seek to do his will on earth. It is our task; we pray for it, and we work for it. In the third sense, we *wait in hope* for its coming, whether by gradual change or by an abrupt termination of earthly history. When it comes, it will signal God's victory over human sin—a victory over all the evil that besets the human spirit, and in the assurance of this victory we find hope.

I believe that Jesus thought of the meaning of the kingdom in all these senses, though with no sharp differentiation among them. The biblical records lend support to all these meanings. As I assess my own understanding of the kingdom, I find myself accepting all three, except for some serious questions about an apocalyptic end of history.

The reader may ask at this point, "What are these questions?" The current widely held belief in an apocalyptic second coming will be given more attention later, but the grounds for questioning it may here be indicated.

In the first place, if the biblical passages affirming the ascension and coming again of Jesus through the clouds are to be taken literally, this runs counter to all we know of astronomy and the space world. This was not a problem for Christians of the first century; it must be for us. We no longer believe that heaven is somewhere up in the sky, and such passages must be demythologized.

As will become more evident in the next chapter, such assumptions were widely current in Jewish eschatology and hence in the currents of opinion within which Jesus lived. So was the idea of Satan as a rival power to God, this being taken over from Persian dualism during the exile. The existence of evil in the world cannot be questioned; the existence of a personal devil and an eternal hell of fire for unbelievers may be.

A third caveat lies in the fact that expectancy of a speedy divine intervention to sweep aside the world's evil tends toward unconcern and inactivity regarding human effort to correct these evils. Much emphasis is placed upon personal salvation to escape divine judgment, and less on making this a better place for all to live in.

An important consideration lies in the fact that the apocalyptic point of view represents only one side of the teaching of Jesus. It has little to say of the conditions of entrance into the kingdom or life within it as these are found elsewhere in the sayings of Jesus, especially in the parables. Thus an emphasis on the second coming as commonly held can lead to bypassing the human situation in major social issues. This is not to charge the exponents of this position with lack of love for other persons, for they often demonstrate a sense of urgency not only to win others to Christ but to be very helpful in immediate personal situations. Yet the same sense of urgency can have, and needs to have, broader foundations.

Finally, much current apocalypticism is drawn from the book of Revelation. This is great poetic drama full of profound meaning in cryptic symbolism, but not written as a chart or charter for our time.

3. A reexamination of the spectrum

With this survey of variant views in the meaning of the kingdom of God as a base of procedure, let us review the types of eschatology that were outlined in the preceding chapter. We shall take them up in the sequence of the previous section.

Weiss and Schweitzer took the third or apocalyptic meaning of the kingdom of God as normative. This led them to assert not only that Jesus expected the imminent and catastrophic end of the world and God's establishment of a new order through his divine messenger, the Son of man, but also that this was the *only* way in which Jesus conceived the kingdom of God. The absoluteness of Jesus' moral demands were then to be understood as an interim ethic before the great cataclysm. They were right in their appreciation of the apocalyptic passages as being in some measure spoken by Jesus. What they failed to do was to give sufficient emphasis to the prophetic teachings and moral commands of Jesus as requisite for the human obligations of the kingdom. Schweitzer in his service to humanity at Lambarene recognized and demonstrated response to these obligations.

The liberal and social gospel theologians chose the second meaning. The kingdom then becomes moral and ethical obedience to God's call within the total sweep of personal and social living, with special emphasis on the human responsibility to correct the evils of an unjust and unloving society. The kingdom of God then becomes the acceptance of the rule of God in the present, with the hope that this may increase through human effort. This was an enormously important emphasis, and I believe it to be not only a much needed but a valid one. Nevertheless, human pride being what it is, some exponents of this prophetic social gospel seemed to lay more stress on the human builders than on the activity of God in the process. Furthermore, a legitimate and needed emphasis on Christian hope got tangled up in a secular evolutionary optimism.

When we come to the "realized eschatology" of C. H. Dodd, we find its chief grounding in the first meaning of the kingdom. Dodd's position, as I understand it, is that Jesus used the phrase "kingdom of God" chiefly in the sense of the eternal, righteous, sovereignty of God and believed that he had been called to manifest this kingdom both supremely and uniquely in his own life and works. Jesus, then, was not announcing a future event when he used the apocalyptic imagery, but symbolized by it the coming of the kingdom in himself. This gives an important emphasis to the fact that there would be no kingdom at all apart from the eternal rulership of God, and no Christian understanding of the kingdom, with its challenge and hope, apart from Christ. It is doubtful that "realized eschatology" is a good name for this point of view, for it suggests that the end of history has already come and minimizes the futuristic element in the thought of Jesus.

The position of Rudolf Bultmann does not fit so readily into any of these three meanings of the kingdom, for his position has elements of all of them. Bultmann's emphasis on existential decision has the eternal and righteous God demanding this decision; it has the critical need of human response, though in a personal rather than social action framework; it has the apocalyptic passages not to be taken literally but as reinforcing the urgency of decision. Yet Bultmann's view that the Gospels almost wholly reflect the thought of the early church shunts us away from forming a judgment of what Jesus himself thought about the kingdom.

In this survey of what I believe the kingdom to be, I have spoken frequently of the effect of the heritage and culture of Jesus upon his thought. To state a composite view, it was not possible to linger at each point to elaborate the nature of this influence. Furthermore, the greatest agreement among scholars is found at the point of their unanimity that the Gospels are colored by the *kerygma*—the preaching and witnessing message of the early church. Thus, we need to look backward from Jesus to his heritage to understand how he came to think as he did about the kingdom of God, and forward from his crucifixion and resurrection to observe how the church dealt with his message. These two large issues will be our next undertaking.

IV
The Kingdom
Before and After Jesus

If we are to arrive with any success at what Jesus believed about the kingdom of God, we must see him as a man of his times who stood within the stream of history. This is not to say that he was *only* a man of his times who tangled with the ruling powers and lost his life as a consequence. Christians through the centuries have rightly designated him as the Christ, the Son of God, the Savior. But this cannot mean that he was not human. To deny the true and full humanity of Jesus was the earliest heresy the church had to confront, and it has persisted to the present. But to make this denial is to reject the incarnation, the cornerstone of Christian faith.

If Jesus were truly a man, and not some mythological supernatural being, he could not fail in some measure to reflect the currents of history. Hence, to examine what he thought about the kingdom, we must note what his fathers thought. We must also try to see in historical perspective what the early church remembered and wrote. Each is a large and very important subject of which this chapter can only trace the outlines.

1. Backgrounds of the kingdom concept

The term "kingdom of God" does not as such appear in the Old Testament. There are many references to earthly kingdoms, as any concordance will indicate, and at three points, in the poetry of Psalms 103:19, 145:11–13, and Daniel 4:3, 34, "his kingdom" or "thy kingdom" in the mood of exalted worship clearly has the Almighty as the antecedent of the pronoun. Thus, we cannot say that the kingdom of God is not mentioned until we come to the New Testament, but as a phrase commonly used it first appears in citations of the words of Jesus.

From the infrequency of the use of this term in the Old Testament we are justified in thinking that Jesus gave it a fresh and original connotation. Furthermore, that this is the product of his own thought, stated at least approximately in his words rather than in the diction of the early church, is borne out by the fact that we find the term used much less frequently in the letters and in Acts than in the Gospels. The memory must have persisted through change.

Yet with little specific reference to the kingdom of God in the Old Testament, its foundations are embedded there. The kingdom concept is rooted in the biblical view of history, with its forward-moving stream of events under the rulership of the sovereign, righteous God. A note which permeates biblical thinking, in contrast with the cyclical or static views often found in other faiths, is that all history moves toward the fulfillment of a divine purpose—toward an end in the double sense of both finish and fulfillment.

The concept of the covenant between God and his chosen people, so dominant in the total history of Israel, underlies this concept of the kingdom. At least from the time of the exodus, with Moses' molding of a tribal people into a nation with a sense of its destiny and a moral consciousness of God's demands, it was the sovereign, righteous rule of God that held them together. Disobey his commands they might, and often did, but Yahweh was still their God and they his people. After the conquest of Canaan and the turmoil of the period of the Judges had given way to a greater degree of stability under the Davidic monarchy, they now had a king, but the Almighty One was still the ultimate sovereign. Earthly fortunes might vacillate, but God

69

never. This was to become more clear-cut as the religious thought of the people moved from *henotheism*—the belief in the existence of other gods but the worship of one only, their own deity—to the outright monotheism affirmed in Isaiah 44:6.

> Thus says the Lord, the King of Israel
> and his Redeemer, the Lord of hosts:
> "I am the first and I am the last;
> besides me there is no god."

Yet though the Lord might be acknowledged as the King of Israel, this was far from ensuring obedience to his sovereignty. There was the downright idolatry of trying to seek favors from Baal, the pagan god of fertility. A ritualistic but shallow worship of Yahweh, also more bent on seeking favors than on rendering homage, became prevalent. To these departures from the true worship of the Most High was joined also a shocking amount of injustice in the oppression of the poor by the rich, the weak by the strong, and the neglect of the needy and the afflicted. This called forth the great social messages of the eighth century prophets—Amos, Hosea, Isaiah, and Micah. We see here the foreshadowing of the thought that the kingdom of God requires social action as well as purity and depth of worship.

It was about this time also that the concept of a future "day of the Lord," which in due time would set everything right, emerged. In general this was thought of as something to antici-pate with eagerness, as the defeat of their enemies and a great benefaction of Yahweh to his chosen people. But Amos thought otherwise and had to blend his message with a darker note. He could say with confidence:

> Seek good, and not evil,
> that you may live;
> and so the Lord, the God of hosts,
> will be with you,
> as you have said. (5:14).

But the other side of God's sovereign rule must also be taken to heart:

> Woe to you who desire the day of the Lord!
>   Why would you have the day of the Lord?
> It is darkness, and not light;
>   as if a man fled from a lion,
>   and a bear met him;
> or went into the house and leaned with
>   his hand against the wall,
>   and a serpent bit him.
> Is not the day of the Lord darkness,
>   and not light,
>   and gloom with no brightness in it? (5:18–20).

It is apparent that the thought which developed later of a great day coming which could bring the joy of God's favor to the righteous and stern judgment on the unrighteous is here in an embryonic state.

Yet though the fortunes of the nation grew steadily worse with inner turmoil and division and with Assyria and Egypt ever in wait to annex the territory (the present Arab-Israeli conflict has a long history!), a note of hope appeared. This was the promise of a Messiah as redeemer and deliverer. This was set forth by one prophet after another. As early as the time of the first Isaiah toward the end of the eighth century we find him saying:

> The people who walked in darkness
>   have seen a great light;
> those who dwelt in a land of deep darkness,
>   on them has light shined (9:2).

This same ninth chapter of Isaiah, which we read so often at Christmas as the annunciation of the coming of Christ—and of which the cadences are woven into our minds through the great music of Handel's *Messiah*—continues with words which bred the belief in a coming political Messiah such as Jesus refused to become. After the words which vividly foretell the coming of a light-bearer such as Christians know Jesus to have been, the passage continues:

> Of the increase of his government and of peace
>   there will be no end,
> upon the throne of David, and over his kingdom,
>   to establish it, and to uphold it
> with justice and with righteousness
>   from this time forth and for evermore.
> The zeal of the Lord of hosts will do this (9:7).

We tend easily to bypass these words, for the throne of David was something of long ago that need not concern us in our day. But not so the people of Isaiah's time, or of several centuries later. One king after another, often very unmessianic in behavior, tried to claim this prerogative. After the conquests by Alexander the Great in 332 B.C., the ensuing domination by the Ptolemies and the Seleucids, and the conquest by Rome under Pompey in 63 B.C. with the annexation of the land as a Roman province, the dream persisted.

While Isaiah confidently foretold the coming of a messianic prince of the house of David, he was nevertheless realistic enough to recognize that Israel, having so woefully broken the people's side of the covenant, would not return as an entire nation to its former greatness. Hence, he announced also the doctrine of the remnant who were to be the custodians of the promise (Isa. 10:20–23).[1] This hope of a righteous remnant continued throughout the exilic and post-exilic periods and on into New Testament times.

Less specifically related to the concept of the kingdom of God in the Old Testament, but very much related to the course which Jesus chose to take, was Jeremiah's vision of the reign of God in the hearts of men. This is a high-water mark of the covenant concept, and of the Old Testament, as the mistrusted and persecuted prophet wrote of the new covenant which would replace the old:

But this is the covenant which I will make with the house of Israel after those days, says the Lord: I will put my law within them, and I will write it upon their hearts; and I will be their God, and they shall be my people. And no longer shall each man teach his neighbor and each his brother, saying "Know the Lord," for they shall all know me, from the least of them to the greatest, says the Lord; for I will forgive their iniquity, and I will remember their sin no more (Jer. 31:33–34).

Ezekiel, after the blow had fallen upon the nation and the exile had destroyed any lingering glory of the house of Israel, portrayed an unquenchable hope in the vision of the valley of dry bones that by the power of God were made to rise up and live again (Ezek. 37:1–14). It was in the words of Ezekiel also that the term "Son of man" became a familiar one. However, as we shall note presently, he was not responsible for giving it the apocalyptic turn that it later came to have.

It was in the great prophet of the exile, Second Isaiah, that the hope of divine deliverance came to its highest expression. It was in a sequence of servant poems, and in particular his portrayal of the Suffering Servant in Isaiah 53, that he set forth at the same time his high hopes for his people and the mode by which God would bring this to pass.

It is generally agreed among biblical scholars that in these servant passages, the prophet was not referring to a particular individual but was calling his people to become the suffering servant of all mankind. Yet the terms in which he describes the servant fit Jesus so aptly that it is more than accidental that Isaiah 53 has often been regarded as a direct prophecy of the coming of Jesus as the Messiah. The fact that Jesus took as the keynote of his ministry the passage in Isaiah 61:1–2 which is quoted in Luke 4:18–19 suggests the depth of the prophet's influence on

73

the formation of Jesus' understanding of his own vocation. Isaiah may have written more prophetically than he knew.

But the people were not able to live up to or out of these great hopes. While the prophets were announcing these great messages of moral responsibility, of impending doom if these were evaded, and of the hope of divine deliverance of the faithful remnant through the coming Messiah, the political fortunes of the people were anything but such as to nourish this hope. The return from exile brought a temporary upturn but no real nationhood, and the subsequent conquests dashed what outward hope there was. Yet the people went on hoping that the coming Messiah would be a political leader who would restore the nation to its former greatness under King David. No wonder that there was consternation, with claims and counterclaims, when Jesus repudiated any aspiration to such a messiahship yet died with an inscription over his head, "This is the King of the Jews" (Luke 23:38). His was a different kind of kingdom, drawn from a new and truer reading of the prophets.

Yet what of the backgrounds of apocalypse? The same troubled times in which the hope of a political Messiah refused to die saw the rise of a different kind of messianic hope. Although the nation's fortunes had seemed to pick up after the return from exile in 538, there was still much internal dissension. After the successive conquests by Alexander's and then by Pompey's legions, what had once been a strong and powerful nation was no nation at all. Yet in those disturbed days, as in ours today, an other-worldly hope grew into prominence as worldly hopes seemed to have less likelihood of fulfillment. God must surely triumph, it was believed, even if not on this sorry earthly plane. His purpose *must* be fulfilled.

It was then that the messianic hope took the form of the expectation of a great, cataclysmic, divine intervention. If no earthly leader were going to come to fulfill the longing of many hearts, one could come from heaven—even down through the clouds! The nation could be lost. This old earth could end. But still one could hope that God would send his Messiah to reign in a new heaven and a new earth. In this new world, with Satan conquered, the righteous would be taken to dwell with the King in a realm of glory, and the wicked would be consigned to eternal punishment. This belief gave assurance of God's justice and his immediacy in both space and time. In a troubled period, it was a needed bulwark to faith and courage.

This heavenly messenger, God's special agent to usher in the new regime at the end of earthly history, came commonly to be spoken of as the Son of man. Furthermore, this end of the world with the day of supernatural deliverance for the faithful could be known to be near at hand. It was to be foreseen by the presence of wars and rumors of war and the presence of many other encompassing evils. In God's own time, the Son of man would come to set up his reign on earth.

But why the Son of *man* rather than of *God*?

The term "Son of man" is used many times in the Old Testament to mean simply "man." It is used with great frequency in Ezekiel, where the context indicates that it means a male human being, but usually with the implication of his being a messenger of God with something of importance to say to the people. In fact, it is Ezekiel's most frequent designation of himself. For example:

And he said to me, "Son of man, stand upon your feet, and I will speak with you." And when he spoke to me, the Spirit entered into me and set me upon my feet; and I heard him speaking to me. And he said to me, "Son of man, I send you to the people of Israel, to a nation of rebels, who have rebelled against me; they and their fathers have transgressed against me to this very day" (2:1–3).

This frequent use of the term in the Old Testament and especially in Ezekiel, who does not hesitate to regard himself as a prophet, throws light on Jesus' frequent use of the term when he refers to himself in connection with his mission. In such passages as "Foxes have holes, and birds of the air have nests; but the Son of man has nowhere to lay his head" (Matt. 8:20) or "the Son of man came eating and drinking, and they say, 'Behold a glutton and a drunkard, a friend of tax collectors and sinners!' " (Matt. 11:19), Jesus is apparently referring to himself in some sense as a special messenger of God, but there is no suggestion here of a supernatural and apocalyptic second coming.

For the apocalyptic connotations of the term "Son of man" we must look to the book of Daniel and the intertestamental writings. Daniel was written in a time of troubles during the persecutions under the Seleucid ruler Antiochus Epiphanes. Its aim was to reinforce the faith of the people. With its setting during the Babylonian captivity under King Nebuchadnezzar four centuries earlier, its primary theme is the divine protection and God-given courage of the fiery furnace and the lion's den. Yet it contains apocalyptic imagery as well. The most influential passage of this type is:

> I saw in the night visions,
>   and behold, with the clouds of heaven
>   there came one like a son of man,
>   and he came to the Ancient of Days
>   and was presented before him.
>   And to him was given dominion
>   and glory and kingdom,
>   that all peoples, nations, and languages
>   should serve him;
>   his dominion is an everlasting dominion,
>   which shall not pass away,
>   and his kingdom one
>   that shall not be destroyed.
>
> (7:13–14. See also verses 9–12.).

What is hinted at here as "one like a son of man" becomes considerably more concrete and definite in the Similitudes of Enoch, where a figure appears who is variously called "the Elect One," or "the Anointed One," or "the Son of man." In him dwells the spirit of wisdom, understanding, and might, and the righteous will remain forever in his presence. He will be God's agent in the day of the Lord—the great day of final victory—and he will "try the works" of the people. At the resurrection of the dead he will winnow out the righteous and take them to dwell with him eternally as he sits on the throne of his glory.

Numerous references to the kingdom of God, or the kingdom of heaven as a reverent way to avoid speaking the divine name, appear in late Jewish literature. Not only I and II Enoch but II Baruch, IV Ezra, the Twelve Testaments, and the Assumption of Moses pave the way for the apocalyptic cosmic drama. In Jewish prayers, the Kaddish, still used today, emerged, "May he establish his kingdom in your lifetime and in your days."

Without specific use of the term "Son of man," an apocalyptic coming of the day of the Lord is indicated elsewhere in the Old Testament as well as in the intertestamental writings. The book of Joel has two dominant themes—the sufferings of the people due to their disobedience, and the imminent day of judgment and hope.

> Blow the trumpet in Zion;
>> sound the alarm on my holy mountain!
> Let all the inhabitants of the land tremble,
>> for the day of the Lord is coming, it is near,
> a day of darkness and gloom,
>> a day of clouds and thick darkness! (Joel 2:1–2).

In great words quoted by Peter at Pentecost the prophet affirms:

> And it shall come to pass afterward,
>> that I will pour out my spirit on all flesh;

> your sons and your daughters shall prophesy,
> your old men shall dream dreams,
> and your young men shall see visions.
> Even upon the menservants and maidservants
> in those days, I will pour out my spirit.
> (Joel 2:28–29. See also Acts 2:17–18.).

The whole book of Zechariah deals with this dual nature of the coming day of the Lord. Here the agency of the Messiah is presupposed, triumphant, and victorious, yet "humble and riding on an ass, on a colt the foal of an ass" (Zech. 9:9. See also Matt. 21:5; John 12:15.). The messianic ruler comes not as a warrior but as a new kind of victor. This may be the background of Jesus' mode of entrance into Jerusalem on Palm Sunday.

In some intertestamental writing the apocalyptic establishment of God's kingdom seems to require no mediator.

> Then His kingdom shall appear throughout all His creation,
> And then Satan shall be no more,
> And sorrow shall depart with him (Assumption of Moses 10:1)[2]

Yet more commonly it is God's chosen messenger who will defeat Satan and bring in the new world that is to come.

The crux of the problem as to the apocalypticism of Jesus and his own relation to the coming kingdom lies in the degree to which he shared this point of view. It is my belief that to some extent he did share it, though he transformed it by an emphasis on the mercy as well as the judgment of God and on the love of God and neighbor as the criterion for God's moral demands. How might he have done so? The Old Testament had not yet been canonized in its present form, and there was no such sharp distinction as the church was later to establish between the sacred writings and others. We have no way of knowing whether Jesus during his hidden years had read these intertestamental writings, especially the passages in the Similitudes of Enoch. Yet this was not impossible, for the book had been written partly in his native Aramaic and partly in Hebrew during the first or second century B.C. Whether or not he had read it, its ideas were in general circulation.

As Jesus pondered the form his own ministry would take, and he became convinced that God had chosen him for a special mission, it was natural enough that he designate himself as the Son of man in the sense in which Ezekiel had used the term. To blend it with the Daniel-Enoch concept was the next step. This he could do so long as he put it in the framework of his own understanding of the love and mercy of God and of moral obedience to the love commandments which God so long before had laid upon his people. And this Jesus appears to have done.

I do not profess to know with certainty that Jesus made this amalgamation. My own faith in him and loyalty to him as the Lord Jesus Christ is in no way dependent on these apocalyptic Son-of-man passages; it hinges upon all that he was and did and said during what we know of his earthly ministry and his continuing presence as the living Christ. It does not impair my confidence in him as, in truth, the unique Son of God and our Savior to think that he may have blended the apocalyptic with the more basic prophetic notes in his ministry.

The third major element in Jesus' legacy from the past is the law. This had been a major element in the entire history of Israel from the time of Moses. The Ten Commandments may have emerged out of the social history of people instead of being dramatically graven on tablets of stone as the first perception of their need; yet God had guided the people in the moral outlook which the commandments embody. Disobeyed again and again, their demands are still relevant. Jesus would never have thought of setting them aside.

The rabbinic literature of Jesus' time shared the eschatological hope of the coming kingdom which has been outlined. But it also reflected a strong sense of divine discipline to be accepted by obedient submission to God's will. The daily repetition of the Shema (Deut. 6:4–5) was regarded as taking upon oneself the yoke of the kingdom. Thus were linked the kingdom and the law. Furthermore, the kingdom was present where the rule of God was obeyed.[3]

Yet over the years, and especially in the later years of Judaism, the law had become cluttered with a great minutia of details—some important to human living, some very trivial. In the time of Jesus, its chief custodians were the Pharisees, who for the most part were good people with whom Jesus had much more in common than with the priestly Sadducees, who were much concerned to preserve their own power and status by currying favor with Rome. Had we a fuller account of the words of Jesus, we might find him saying better things of the Pharisees than those which have led us to think unkindly of them. Yet as prophecy had declined, the law had tended to become externalized; its letter rather than its spirit was accented. Jesus did not hesitate to disregard the sabbath observance and the dietary regulations when they conflicted with human good or to point out the hypocrisy latent in such legalism.

Jesus took the law seriously, not to abolish but to fulfill it (Matt. 5:17), and this too enters as a legacy from the past into his concept of the kingdom. In his summary of the demands of personal living as these are epitomized in the Beatitudes and illustrated again and again in his parables of the kingdom, the moral law is not left behind but its external demands are turned inward. Here we have again, though in a different framework, the new covenant written in the hearts of men which Jeremiah had announced so long before. And with it is blended the way of self-denial, of self-giving, and of service which was to become the way of the Cross.

This approach through the law is less obviously related to Jesus' understanding of the kingdom than the approach through either prophecy or apocalypse. Yet it was to bear much fruit, for he had an encompassing sense of the importance of moral obedience to the will of God as a condition of entrance into the kingdom. The call to put the love of God and neighbor above legalistic requirements was basic to his message. But his concern for the law persisted in his summons to distinguish between the external obedience required by it and the inner fidelity to a higher law required of a life reborn by the love and mercy of God. This distinction was to become in Paul's thought a sharp distinction between the law and the gospel, with the gospel centered in Jesus himself. To Jesus, the good news God had commissioned him to announce was the higher law of love, and its expression was an indispensable requirement of entrance into the kingdom of God.

If these antecedents from his heritage were present in the mind of Jesus, as it seems certain that they were, it is not surprising that they should have found their way into his understanding and speaking of the kingdom. Indeed, it would have been surprising if they had not. The marvel is that he took them and so transformed them that their major notes have continued to be vital and compelling to the present day. In this lies his uniqueness and his Saviorhood.

If this be the case, then an understanding of the kingdom in three senses—the eternal, righteous rule of the sovereign God; the call to moral obedience in love; and an apocalyptic final consummation—seems less inconsistent in the thought of Jesus than they have often been assumed to be. As he pondered the nature of his ministry at the call of God, it is not surprising that he should have expected an imminent end of the present world and believed that God had called him to be the harbinger of judgment and salvation.

2. Did Jesus believe himself to be the Messiah?

Did Jesus believe that he was the promised Messiah? This is a question on which competent scholars are not agreed. Among those who answer the question in the affirmative, there is still not full agreement as to how he conceived the messiahship. The question has been presupposed in what has been said up to this point, but the antecedents of the issue needed to be stated before considering it directly.

This author's position is that it depends on the meaning given to the term. Then some things can be said with certainty, others only tentatively.

It seems clear that Jesus rejected outright the historic, and in his time the most common, understanding of the Messiah as a political deliverer who would restore Israel to its former greatness under King David. The Zealots sought the fulfillment of this hope by trying by force of arms to throw off the Roman yoke. While this was primarily a revolutionary effort of irreconcilable patriots rather than a messianic movement, they would doubtless have been glad to claim Jesus as their leader. He refused any overtures they may have made. Although Simon the Zealot (so called to distinguish him from Simon Peter) was one of the disciples (Luke 6:15; Acts 1:13), he does not figure prominently in the Gospel narrative, and there is no convincing evidence that Jesus had anything to do with the Zealot movement. At the beginning of his ministry his resistance to the temptations to claim for himself economic, political, or personal supernatural power may well reflect an inner struggle over the issue. If so, then the outcome was a complete repudiation of the political messianic hope. One of the disciples could say sadly after his crucifixion, "But we had hoped that he was the one to redeem Israel" (Luke 24:21). Yet this seems never to have been the hope of Jesus in the sense in which the disciple conceived it. [4]

But did Jesus believe himself to be the Son-of-man Messiah? Here the affirmative evidence is stronger, and we have noted that he made much of this Son-of-man terminology, or so the record indicates. He speaks of himself repeatedly as Son of man in the prophetic sense in which Ezekiel had used the term, and numerous passages suggest that the final consummation will be ushered in by the apocalyptic coming of the Son of man. Yet on further examination it does not appear that he is necessarily referring to himself. For example:

When they persecute you in one town, flee to the next; for truly, I say to you, you will not have gone through all the towns of Israel, before the Son of man comes (Matt. 10:23).

For the Son of man is to come with his angels in the glory of his Father, and then he will repay every man for what he has done. Truly, I say to you, there are some standing here who will not taste death before they see the Son of man coming in his kingdom (Matt. 16:27–28).

For as the lightning comes from the east and shines as far as the west, so will be the coming of the Son of man (Matt. 24:27).

When the Son of man comes in his glory, and all the angels with him, then he will sit on his glorious throne (Matt. 25:31).

Therefore you also must be ready; for the Son of man is coming at an hour you do not expect (Matt. 24:44).

Whether Jesus in such passages was speaking of himself or of a heavenly being known only as the Son of man, the early church was so convinced that Jesus was the Messiah that they made this identification.[5] Jesus apparently believed in an imminent end of the present age. That he thought of himself as coming again in so dramatic a manner is less certain. By the time of the writing of John's Gospel toward the end of the century, the dominant note had become the promise of the indwelling Holy Spirit that would succeed him to guide his followers in ways of truth and service.

The most we can say with certainty at this point is that Jesus may have thought of himself as the Messiah in the Son-of-man sense, and that his first century followers believed he had repeatedly made this claim. But this does not end the inquiry.

We have noted that the Old Testament prophet on whom Jesus seems most to have patterned his life work was the one whom he knew as Isaiah, though we may now speak of him as Second Isaiah, since he wrote during the exile and about one hundred and fifty years after the Isaiah of the eighth century. What Jesus sought to be and to do, at the call of God, was to give himself in suffering love to his people and to all whom he could serve and redeem by the power of God.

Does this mean that Jesus believed he was the expected Messiah? Here the lines of distinction become tenuous, for while the words of Isaiah were familiar enough, there was no "suffering servant Messiah" in the expectation of the people. There are two ways of putting what seems to have been Jesus' understanding of his calling. We can say that he believed himself to be the Messiah but with a fresh understanding of all that the term implied.[6] Or we can say that he believed God had given him a unique vocation—to manifest and to establish the reign of God on earth through a ministry of service and self-giving love.

Actually, these are two ways of saying the same thing, though they elicit differing emotional and theological connotations. The early church was certain that in Jesus we see "the Christ, the Son of the living God" (Matt. 16:16). This conviction has been transmitted by the scriptures, tradition, and experience to the present day. I believe this designation to be meaningful and true, provided we do not distort it to the point of denying the humanity of Jesus and with it the incarnation.

Yet this still does not answer the question as to whether Jesus believed he was the Christ. Since the words directly following Peter's affirmation in Matthew 16:16 refer to the church, which did not exist in Jesus' lifetime, the passage may be an interpolation from early Christian thought. Jesus was addressed as "Good Teacher," and we have the rejoinder, "Why do you call me good? No one is good but God alone" (Mark 10:18. See also Luke 18:19.). When during his trial he was asked by the governor, "Are you the King of the Jews?" the reply is simply, "You have said so" (Matt. 27:11). In Luke the question is, "Are you the Son of God, then?" and the answer is equivocal, "You say that I am" (Luke 22:70). It is only in Mark that we find a clear affirmative. In reply to the high priest's question, "Are you the Christ, the Son of the Blessed?" the answer is, "I am; and you will see the Son of man seated at the right hand of Power, and coming with the clouds of heaven" (Mark 14:61–62).[7]

So, perhaps we had best conclude that we cannot enter Jesus' own consciousness to say with certainty just how he thought of himself in relation to the ancient messianic hope. We *can* be sure that he had no doubt of having been called by God to a special mission for the redemption of his own people, and beyond them of all humanity. Whether or not he accepted for himself the the title of the Christ, the Anointed One, we are fully justified in using it.

3. The kingdom of God in the early church

A point on which biblical scholars are agreed is that in the preaching and teaching of the apostolic church, it was Jesus himself as Christ the Lord, the Son of God, the Savior that became the central message. In fact, the *ichthus* or "fish," which became the sacred symbol found repeatedly on the walls of the catacombs where the persecuted Christians took refuge, is an acronym formed from the first letters of the Greek words for "Jesus Christ, Son of God, Savior." The kingdom of God is referred to in Paul's letters, the book of Acts, and elsewhere, but much less attention is given to it than to Christ, the crucified and risen Lord. The fact that it is so central in the Synoptic Gospels, which were compiled considerably later than any of Paul's letters, is evidence that the kingdom teachings of Jesus had persisted in spite of, and perhaps because of, the centrality given to Jesus as the Christ.

Enough has been said of Jesus' teaching about the kingdom of God as presented in the Synoptic Gospels so that we need not linger in repetition of it. However, some significant aspects may be indicated. The first of these is that the lapse of time between the death of Jesus and the writing of Mark, the earliest Gospel, may have modified but did not quench the memory of this teaching. It must be authentic in its general structure, or it would not have been preserved. The second is to call attention to the fact that Matthew, and he only, used "the kingdom of heaven" as a synonym for "the kingdom of God," and does so some thirty times. The probable reason is that this author was writing primarily for the church that was centered in Jerusalem, and the Jews had long hesitated to speak the name of God openly, lest in doing so they profane him in violation of the third commandment. A third matter of note is that Luke freely includes references to the kingdom in citing the sayings of Jesus, though less often than Matthew, but in the book of Acts by the same author the references to the kingdom are few. This seems to indicate that he could not tell the story of Jesus without them, though in the early church this note had become subordinate to Jesus himself as the Christ.

In the Gospel of John we find a very different approach. Its purpose is stated succinctly by its author, "these are written that you may believe that Jesus is the Christ, the Son of God, and that believing you may have life in his name" (20:31). Though it contains great, tender words about life after death, its primary concern is not eschatology but eternal life through Christ in the

present. It has no apocalyptic language and only a brief reference, in what is probably a later addition, to Christ's return
(21:22). Instead, the Holy Spirit will come as the counselor to
teach them all things and keep fresh his memory (14:26).[8]

Prominent as is the teaching of the kingdom in the Synoptics,
in John it is found only twice and this in a single passage. In the
interview with Nicodemus, Jesus says, "Truly, truly, I say to
you, unless one is born anew, he cannot see the kingdom of
God." When Nicodemus asks how this can be, the reply becomes more specific, "Truly, truly, I say to you, unless one is
born of water and the Spirit, he cannot enter the kingdom of
God" (John 3:3, 5). This suggests that by the end of the first
century, when John's Gospel was written, both baptism as the
external sign of regeneration and the Holy Spirit as its inner
agency had become linked to the concept of the kingdom. But of
the kingdom itself we hear no more in the fourth Gospel. John,
like the other three evangelists, accents the importance of the
crucifixion and resurrection by giving these events a major place
in the narrative; but unlike them he makes the divinity of Jesus
so predominant over his humanity that the teachings presented
take quite a different turn.

In John there is no agony in Gethsemane, no cry of dereliction
from the Cross, but Jesus is in complete command of every
situation. This brings about in the trial scene an indirect reference to the kingdom in a different context from that in the
Synoptics. When asked by Pilate, "Are you the King of the
Jews?" Jesus answers, "My kingship is not of this world; . . .
For this I was born, and for this I have come into the world, to
bear witness to the truth. Every one who is of the truth hears my
voice" (18:36–37). The kingship of Jesus, not a kingdom to be
entered, is here the central note.

In Acts we are told that Jesus continued to speak of the
kingdom in his post-resurrection appearances (1:3). Yet the

difficulty encountered by even his closest disciples to grasp his message is evidenced by the fact that when they came together they asked him, "Lord, will you at this time restore the kingdom to Israel?" The Davidic Messiah was still their dream! Jesus apparently thought that it was useless to argue with them, for he told them it was not for them to know the times or seasons fixed by the Father's authority. Instead, they should be witnesses to him by the power of the Holy Spirit "in Jerusalem and in all Judea and Samaria and to the end of the earth" (1:6–8).

In Luke's account of the birth and spread of the church in Acts, we find a few references to the kingdom of God, first in connection with Philip's and then with Paul's preaching and teaching about the kingdom (8:12; 14:22; 19:8; 28:23, 31). What they indicate is that the kingdom message was not forgotten, but was not taken nearly so seriously as the impulse to preach Christ crucified and the good news of salvation through Christ. The references are very general, the most concrete being the statement that in Lystra, Iconium, and Antioch Paul and Barnabas were "strengthening the souls of the disciples, exhorting them to continue in the faith, and saying that through many tribulations we must enter the kingdom of God" (Acts 14:22).

In Paul's letters there are more references to the kingdom of God than in Acts, but considering the volume of the letters the proportion is no greater. Paul clearly believed in an imminent end of the present world. Yet it is noteworthy that he does not associate it with any such dramatic panoply as the Synoptic Gospels were later to present. While the term "second coming," in so many words, is found nowhere in the New Testament, there are brief references to the Lord's coming in I Corinthians 4:5 and 15:23; I Thessalonians 2:19, 4:15, and 5:23; and a day of judgment through Christ in Romans 2:16. These are similar to somewhat incidental references in John 21:22, James 5:7, and Revelation 2:25. It would appear that these writers, in common with the prevalent idea in the early church, believed that Christ would return, but they stopped short of making this a spectacular event.

Paul seems to have thought of the kingdom as both present and future, and what is dominant in his mention of it is a strong emphasis on its moral requirements. We are told in Romans 14:17, "For the kingdom of God is not food and drink but righteousness and peace and joy in the Holy Spirit." Again in I Corinthians 4:20 in a protest against too much arrogant talk we find Paul saying, "For the kingdom of God does not consist in talk but in power." The futuristic element blends with the moral as he says in I Corinthians 6:9, "Do you not know that the unrighteous will not inherit the kingdom of God?" Then he proceeds to give a list of offenses which mark the unrighteous. There is a similar approach in Galatians 5:19–21 with a long list of offenses. Yet the passage leads into his priceless statement, "But the fruit of the Spirit is love, joy, peace, patience, kindness, goodness, faithfulness, gentleness, self-control; against such there is no law" (5:22–23). Apparently these are the qualities most basic for membership in the kingdom of God.

In a few passages Paul speaks of the kingdom of Christ. In Ephesians 5:5, if he wrote this letter, Paul has it that no immoral or impure man "has any inheritance in the kingdom of Christ and of God." In a more authentic but also more obscure passage in I Corinthians 15:23–28 he speaks of the coming of Christ and says, "Then comes the end, when he delivers the kingdom to God the Father after destroying every rule and every authority and power. For he must reign until he has put all his enemies under his feet" (15:24–25). There seems here to be a blend of the present reign of Christ before the final consummation with an ultimate surrender to God of the authority delegated to him as the Christ.

What shall we make of all this? What I make of it has already been indicated along the way, but a summary may be in order. This is that Jesus was heavily indebted to his past, but was no copyist of it; that he spoke as an apocalyptist, but that his apocalypticism was probably distorted and exaggerated in the records of the Synoptics; more important, that he had a prophetic sense of mission as God's suffering servant and agent of redemption; that he deeply respected the law of his fathers, but gave it a new depth of meaning in self-giving love. I believe with his followers in the early church that Jesus was the Christ, the Son of the living God, and our Savior; and that he believed himself to have a unique calling and God-given mission. To Jesus the kingdom of God was the universal, eternal, righteous reign of God, only partially accepted amid the world's evil yet a present fact, a sphere of human existence to be entered and furthered by moral obedience in love to the will of God. He believed also in a final consummation with God's victory over evil, and believed himself to be God's agent in bringing this to pass. Whether this is equivalent to saying that he believed himself to be the Messiah depends on the connotation given to this term.

The reader is invited to agree or to disagree with these conclusions to the degree that the evidence that has been presented seems persuasive. However, they will be presupposed in the remainder of the book.

V
The Kingdom
in the Parables

As any good concordance will indicate, many references to the kingdom of God are ascribed to Jesus in the Synoptic Gospels. On the basis of these sayings it is possible by some selectivity to defend any of the four major types of understanding of the kingdom outlined in chapter 2. Taken collectively they justify what was affirmed in chapter 3 as primary notes in the meaning of the term: the ultimate sovereignty of God; the acceptance of this sovereignty through human response and obedience to God's will; and a final, victorious consummation of the total process. Thus the kingdom is above, within, and at the end of human history, with the end meaning both goal and fulfillment.

These notes I believe to have been basic to the thought of Jesus, which he conceived as a whole without any one, two, three or abc differentiations. But stated thus for theological analysis, the concept still lacks concreteness. This concreteness Jesus supplied for his own time in the parables, and if we can discern the timeless meaning in these matchless stories, we are in a better position to find it for our own.

1. Why the parables?

And what is a parable? It is neither a simple figure of speech nor an allegory, which is sometimes confused with it. An allegory is an extended simile in narrative form with a point for point meaning to be drawn from each of its parts. A parable is a short story drawn from common life which is intended to convey a moral or religious truth. Each parable has a single focus, and distortion occurs when we try to treat it as an allegory.

The parables of Jesus have special importance to our theme for several reasons. In the first place, they are probably the most authentic of all the sayings ascribed to Jesus. This is not to say that we have here a stenographic, verbatim account of just what he said. Yet, based as they were in familiar life situations, they were easy to remember. They were doubtless told again and again in the early church, as today one remembers the illustrations in a sermon, and thus found their way into not only the oral tradition of the church but the earlier written sources of the Gospels. We may perhaps question some of the interpretations inserted by the Gospel writers, but there is no serious reason to doubt that in the main the parables themselves are authentic.

A second reason for the importance of the parables is their uniqueness, which gives further evidence of their originality. In the Old Testament there are allegories, fables, and plenty of similes and metaphors, but only two real parables: Nathan's story of the poor man's one ewe lamb (II Sam. 12:1–6) and Isaiah's parable of the unproductive vineyard (Isa. 5:1–7). In the New Testament they are found only in the Synoptic Gospels. With such metaphors in John as the "bread of life" and "vine and branches," these passages lack the narrative quality which would make them parables. There is some difference of opinion among scholars as to whether stories found in rabbinic writings before the time of Jesus constitute parables, but no less an authority than Joachim Jeremias makes this positive statement, "Jesus' parables are something entirely new. In all the rabbinic literature, not one single parable has come down to us from the period before Jesus." He says further that in comparison with Paul's similitudes and the rabbinic parables that appeared later, the parables of Jesus are distinctly different. "Comparison reveals a definite personal style, a singular clarity and simplicity, a matchless mastery of construction. The conclusion is inevitable that we are dealing with particular trustworthy tradition. We are standing right before Jesus when reading his parables."[1]

An element in the nature of this difference has a bearing on the message of Jesus as a whole, and the kingdom in particular, and thus forms a third reason for their importance. Jesus loved nature and thought of everything in nature as made by God and part of God's good world. One looks in vain in Paul for any such sensitivity to nature's beauty or the goodness of small things throughout God's creation. Says C. H. Dodd, the other major exponent of the parables:

This sense of the divineness of the natural order is the major premise of all the parables, and it is the point where Jesus differs most profoundly from the outlook of the Jewish apocalyptists, with whose ideas He had on some sides much sympathy. The orthodox Rabbis of the Talmud are also largely free from the gloomy pessimism of apocalypse; . . . but their minds are more scholastic, and their parables often have a larger element of artificiality than those of the Gospels.[2]

A fourth reason, already intimated, for giving special attention to the parables is that they reflect the bearing of the kingdom on the conditions of everyday living in human relations. The setting, to be sure, is first century rural Galilee with its small towns and open farm and grazing land rather than contemporary urban America. Jesus never gives us abstract theologizing about the nature of the kingdom. But here we see what the kingdom means for daily living in terms of its worth which calls forth quest, the conditions of its entrance, the call to continuing obedience, and the assurance of divine control and concern which undergird hope.

In what follows, no attempt will be made to cover the more than forty parables which are found in the Gospels. Those which will be looked at bear most directly on Jesus' understanding of the kingdom. Some of them state this directly in such words as "The kingdom of heaven is like. . . ." In others the relation is only by implication. Some of them seem to contradict each other. Yet if what is looked for in them is not logical consistency but a life setting that deals both with existence in the kingdom in the present and an expectation of its coming, there is wholeness and unity. What I shall aim to do in this chapter is call attention to this unity which becomes more evident as the parables are viewed together, but from several angles of Jesus' thought.

2. The worth of the kingdom

Jesus never leaves his hearers in any doubt of the supreme worth of the kingdom to their lives. This is evident from its centrality in his total message. Its superiority to physical needs, even to very real ones for which God has concern, is expressed clearly in the Sermon on the Mount (Matt. 6:25–33). Its antithesis to the lust for material gain comes out in the striking hyperbole which loses all its meaning if it is lamely literalized. "It is easier for a camel to go through the eye of a needle than for a rich man to enter the kingdom of God" (Matt. 19:24. See also Mark 10:25 and Luke 18:25.).

Particular references to the worth of the kingdom are fewer and briefer in the parables than to other angles of it, though it is presupposed in all of them. Perhaps Jesus took this for granted and felt no need to keep talking about it. Its explicit affirmation is limited to two verses in Matthew 13:44–45.

The kingdom of heaven is like treasure hidden in a field, which a man found and covered up; then in his joy he goes and sells all that he has and buys that field.

Again, the kingdom of heaven is like a merchant in search of fine pearls, who, on finding one pearl of great value, went and sold all that he had and bought it.

Both these parables have their setting in the Galilee of Jesus' day. Burying a treasure in order to guard its safety was a natural thing to do when the houses and shops had flimsy walls and insecure doors, and there were no bank vaults. "The protection of wealth by burying it in the ground was a sort of ancient equivalent for the modern safety deposit box." [3] Though it is unlikely that buying pearls was a common practice in Jesus' home or among his neighbors, there were undoubtedly pearl merchants among the caravans that came through on the well-traveled road between Damascus and Egypt.

It is easy to raise some puzzling questions about these two swift glimpses into the mind of Jesus. What about the honesty of finding another's hidden treasure, carefully concealing it from everybody, and then by buying the field making a good rake-off at the owner's expense? Is Jesus trying to tell us to throw prudence to the winds and sink everything in one deal? We have seen this work havoc and cause long drawn-out suffering that could hardly be God's will.

Doubtless there were dishonest and imprudent people in Jesus' time, but here he is not trying either to commend or to rebuke them. Let us remember that a parable is intended to convey only one point and not try to allegorize it by reading extraneous matter into it. With this procedure it is clear that the point in both these parables is not something about economic ethics. It is the supreme worth of the kingdom of God and hence the need to orient one's life and dedicate one's self completely toward this goal. [4]

But what is this goal? It is the supremacy of love in all of life, for God is love. To be sure, no mention is made of love in this particular passage. But we cannot leave it out when the life, the ministry, and the message of Jesus are so completely centered in it. Life in the kingdom has no place for halfway measures; it costs all that we have, and this supreme requirement is the love of God and neighbor. We enter the kingdom by accepting God's rule and with it the demands of love in all our relationships.

The unfinished tower and the king going to war without counting the cost is another pair of parables accenting the worth of the kingdom. They appear only in Luke 14:25–33, but with a tangent passage in Matthew as Jesus gives instruction to his disciples (10:34–39). The dominant note is the call to complete self-renunciation if one would become a disciple, hence the worth of that to which Jesus summons his followers. These parables expand and supplement the message of the treasure hidden in the field and the pearl of great value and form a corrective if one is needed. Should one assume from these briefer parables that joyous possession makes no further demands, this error is here decisively corrected. However essential the first step, it is never enough. Evangelism in both the conventional and the charismatic churches of our time might be greatly vitalized if this were taken more seriously.

But are not the demands too severe? And what about love? Can we suppose God requires a Christian to "hate his own father and mother and wife and children and brothers and sisters, yes, and even his own life" (Luke 14:26)? Again we see the perils of literalism. More than a few in Christian history have felt impelled by these words to sever their family ties, with the result of cruelty to those nearest and otherwise dearest, sometimes with the distortion of their own personalities. Granted that a hard decision must sometimes be made between loyalty to family and loyalty to some other God-given duty, we cannot suppose that the God of infinite love asks us to disregard human love and its obligations. What Jesus seems to be saying here, again in a striking hyperbole that his hearers would have understood perhaps better than we, is that his followers must ever be on guard lest a human good draw us away from following the highest goodness.

What of the mockery that ensues when one starts to build a tower and is unable to finish it? Since the Greek word for tower can mean any high or expensive building, it is a synonym for anything important. But it is concrete imagery that is not basic to the parable. The point still holds that acceptance of the rule of God is of supreme importance even if retreat brings not mockery but approval, as it often does in current secular society. Such approval is apt to increase the difficulty of authentic discipleship, and elsewhere Jesus gives the warning, "Woe to you, when all men speak well of you" (Luke 6:26). Whether mockery or popularity results from retreat, the cost of discipleship is steadfastness in bearing the obligations of the rule of God.

Nor should the common tendency to allegorize mislead us in what Jesus says about the king's inadequate preparation for war. This is not designed to be an argument for military preparedness! On Palm Sunday morning Jesus wept over Jerusalem because the people knew not the things that make for peace (Luke 19:41–42). But in driving home a point he adopts a setting for it with which they are all familiar. The point is the costing nature of membership in a higher kingdom than that of any earthly power.

Luke places directly after these parables the word about the savorless salt, with which Matthew ends the Beatitudes. Its meaning is clear enough to sting. One way in which the judgment of God works is that inner depreciation of selfhood which comes from surrendering high goals for low and self-centered aims.

3. The conditions of entrance

The parables already glanced at give witness not only to the supreme worth of the kingdom but to its cost in self-dedication. This is the primary and inclusive condition of entrance into and of life within it; that is, of living a Christian life. But at once the question arises, "Is complete self-dedication ever possible?" There are those in our time as in the past who hold that when radical conversion is followed by sanctification, now more commonly called the baptism of the Spirit, Christian perfection ensues. An honest look within, even to say nothing of the fruits observed in the lives of others, makes this a very doubtful conclusion. Being finite and fallible human beings, we need to guard against the conclusion that there is no self-centeredness left in us.

Yet what is possible is to make self-dedication to the rule and will of God a matter of firm decision and a lifetime goal. This seems to be what Jesus meant by entrance into the kingdom of God. And to do this, certain attitudes are essential. Foremost among these are faith, repentance, and humility.

Faith requires trust in God and the recognition that our ultimate destiny is in God's hands. The kingdom of God is God's gift, not a human achievement. It is God's initiative, born of the love that is the source of divine grace, which opens the kingdom to all believers—which is to say, to those who will meet the conditions for entrance into it.

Such faith is basic to the doctrine of justification by faith, which was first spelled out by Paul and never stated by Jesus in theological terms, yet was presupposed in all he said about the kingdom of God. It is to distort it and advocate what Dietrich Bonhoeffer in a now classic term has called "cheap grace" if no human cost is taken into account.[5] Yet to assume that we "build the kingdom" is equally a distortion.

The parables which best illustrate the divine initiative that stems from the yearning love of God for every person, whatever one's moral status or station in life, are the trilogy of the lost sheep, the lost coin, and the lost boy, ordinarily called the prodigal son. Whether the three were spoken by Jesus in quick succession we do not know, but Luke's arrangement of them in chapter 15, constituting the entire chapter, places them in an arresting juxtaposition. The first two have the same point, but since the third deals specifically with a human situation it takes a somewhat different turn.

The stories gather meaning if seen in their setting (Luke 15:1, 2). The preaching of Jesus was attracting tax collectors and sinners, and he was even eating with them, which was shocking to the respectable religious leaders of his time. To eat together has long been a primary symbol of fellowship and hence of division when a cleavage, racial or religious, intervenes. The Pharisees and scribes were much disturbed, and these parables are Jesus' answer.

The point is clear that God is eternally seeking to save the lost, and the sinner is as much the object and recipient of the love of God as the righteous. This is both the ground of our faith and the solvent of man-made cleavages. These parables vividly affirm God's concern for all persons, whatever their goodness or badness or station in life. On this certainty we can rest our faith.

The third parable accents most the need of repentance, though joy over the penitent sinner appears in all. A sheep or a coin cannot repent, but a son can, and his repentance is spelled out dramatically. Here is clearly suggested the need of appropriate human response as well as of divine caring. It was when the boy "came to himself" and said, "I will arise and go to my father," that he found himself willing to say, "Father, I have sinned against heaven and before you; I am no longer worthy to be called your son" (Luke 15:17–19). It was then that the redemption took place.

There is no specific mention of the kingdom in connection with these parables. Yet they are nonetheless parables of the kingdom, and the call to repentance is sounded so often elsewhere that we must believe Jesus considered it a basic condition of entrance. It begins in Mark with the preaching of John the

Baptist and quickly appears in the message of Jesus. "Now after John was arrested, Jesus came into Galilee, preaching the gospel of God, and saying, 'The time is fulfilled, and the kingdom of God is at hand; repent, and believe in the gospel' " (Mark 1:14). The call to repentance continues thoroughly through the Synoptics, drops out in John, and reappears in full force in Acts and the Letters. It must have been a dominant note in the thought of the early church.

To comment on our current situation, the failure to take sin seriously and with it the need for repentance is one of the major weaknesses of modern society and with it the modern church. This is not to say that sin and penitence are the only notes that need to be sounded; there is need of a positive upbuilding of personality. Yet to a great extent either conventional decency or psychological adjustment has become the goal most put forward, with little sense of the need of recognizing one's guilt before God. So serious is this and so adverse to full personhood that the nation's outstanding psychiatrist, Karl Menninger, has recently written a book with the arresting title, *Whatever Became of Sin?*[6]

Because God is supremely good, our sin matters greatly in the sight of God. Though repentance can never assure us of moral perfection, it is a prime requisite to the obedience demanded by God's sovereign rule. But it is not the only requirement.

That penitence and humility are closely linked is evident in the familiar parable of the Pharisee and the publican (Luke 18:9-14). The Pharisee was no doubt a good man. Most of them were, in spite of the invectives found in Matthew 23 which have given them a bad reputation. The trouble was that they were too well aware of their own virtue and did not hesitate self-righteously to announce it. As for the tax collector, he may or may not have feathered his nest in collecting the taxes—Jesus is not discussing the nature of his infractions—but he had the honesty and the humility to say, "God, be merciful to me a sinner!" and to open his soul to the grace of God.

This parable appears only in Luke, but immediately after it stands an incident which is a parable in action and which has been preserved also in Matthew and Mark (Luke 18:15–17; Matt. 19:13–15; Mark 10:13–16). This is the bringing of little children to Jesus that he might touch them, somewhat as people today like to have a political candidate kiss their babies. When the disciples rebuked them, he rebuked the disciples. "Let the children come to me, and do not hinder them; for to such belongs the kingdom of God. Truly, I say to you, whoever does not receive the kingdom of God like a child shall not enter it." This, of course, does not mean childishness, but a childlike openness and trust.

The theme of humility appears again in the parable of the chief seats at the wedding supper. The pretentious must take a back seat while the humble are called to a higher station (Luke 14:7–11). Jesus with prophetic intensity condemns any act that is ostensibly religious but has as its main incentive human approval. The severity of the woes pronounced upon the scribes and Pharisees in Matthew 23 may have become exaggerated in the transcribing. (I am inclined to think they were, but they are a true enough reflection of what Jesus thought about religious pretense and hypocrisy.) Hence, the need of humility, openness, and sincerity if one would find a place in the kingdom of God.

4. Life in the kingdom

No sharp distinction can be drawn between the requirements of coming into the kingdom of God and those of life within it. The Christian life, like any other, experiences change, but change within continuity. Yet life within the kingdom, or the accepted sovereignty of God, has in it an important note sometimes underprized by those who place primary stress on a radical conversion. This is the call to sensitivity and service to every human need.

Foremost among the parables which emphasize this aspect of life in the kingdom is the familiar parable of the Good Samaritan (Luke 10:25–37). With a clarity not easily misunderstood, it begins with a restatement of the two great commandments, then gives a graphic picture of neighborliness in a situation of response to human need that transcends any man-made lines of division. Christians have often failed to act in accord with it, but seldom if ever does one question its authenticity to the mind and spirit of Jesus.

With much the same thrust, despite its linkage with an apocalyptic concept of divine judgment, is the presentation of the separation of the sheep from the goats in the last judgment (Matt. 25:31–46). One's place in the kingdom is then to be determined by his ministry to the hungry, the thirsty, the stranger, the naked, the imprisoned. The King will say, "'Truly, I say to you, as you did it to one of the least of these my brethren, you did it to me.'" It is not clear whether Jesus is here identifying himself with the King or expected Messiah, but it *is* clear that here he discloses his interests and priorities with an unmistakable directive for life in the kingdom. Strictly speaking, this is an apocalypse rather than a parable, but it has great value in showing that to Jesus an apocalyptic kingdom would be meaningless without human service as its precondition.

There is a trilogy of parables given in rapid succession in each of the three Gospels, and surprisingly in the same order, which does not often occur. These are the parables of the wedding guests who need not fast while the bridegroom is with them; of putting a new patch on an old garment; and of putting new wine in old wineskins (Matt. 9:14–17; Mark 2:18–22; Luke 5:33–39). The setting given applies to all of them. The disciples of John and the Pharisees were fasting; those of Jesus were not. The people wanted to know, "Why so?" The reply of Jesus by the three parables suggests the need of freshness, vitality, authenticity of personal experience in contrast with a mere maintenance of traditional patterns. But note that Jesus does not say that the innovative should be sought simply because it is new, or that life should be celebrated in a service of worship simply for enjoyment.

5. The parables of growth

Turning to the parables of growth, we find a number of them. But these are not parables of the individual's growth in the Christian life. This was not the familiar concept then that it is today and was not accented by Jesus; nor in the Bible as a whole, though we find suggestions of it in the Letters in injunctions to "grow up in every way into him who is the head, into Christ" (Eph. 4:15) and to "grow in the grace and knowledge of our Lord and Savior Jesus Christ" (II Pet. 3:18). It is not surprising that in a time when there was no such knowledge of the processes of human development as we now have, little attention was given to what we must now consider vital to Christian nurture.

Yet there are important parables of growth which the evangelists have given us as spoken by Jesus. They refer to a corporate increase in acceptance of his message, and hence a growing response to the kingly rule of God. Matthew has arranged them together in chapter 13, each preceded by "The kingdom of heaven is like" or some equivalent phrase. There we find the parables of the sower, the tares, the mustard seed, and the leaven (Matt. 13:18–33) Mark alone has a fifth in the earth bearing fruit of itself (4:26–29). The sower and the mustard seed are in all three Gospels; the leaven in Matthew and Luke; and the tares in Matthew only. This amount of inclusion indicates that all the evangelists took seriously the parables of growth.

To see to what these parables were pointing, it is necessary to take into account the situation within which the evangelists compiled them in the latter part of the first century. The church by this time had grown considerably, and no clear distinction was drawn between the church and the kingdom. Even though it was recognized that the time of the coming of the kingdom was in God's hands, it would not have occurred to these writers that the kingdom could come apart from the church. Yet it had become evident that within the church, as within the world, there were both wheat and tares, good people and bad, and this had brought to the fore the issue of weeding out evil elements. Furthermore, the expected end of the world with a catastrophic last judgment had not occurred; some explanation needed to be found and encouragement given as the waiting continued.

The parables of growth were an answer to these problems. This is not to infer that the writers made them up and then attributed them to Jesus. There is as good reason to suppose that these were in the oral and written sources as any of the others. But the evangelists apparently adapted them to their times. In the process the parables of the sower and the tares became allegories, with extended point for point explanations added which probably were not in the words of Jesus.

This process of addition and adaptation may explain why Mark at the end of the sower parable, but before its explanation, includes some cryptic words attributed to Jesus explaining why he spoke in parables. "To you has been given the secret of the kingdom of God, but for those outside everything is in parables; so that they may indeed see but not perceive, and may indeed hear but not understand; lest they should turn again, and be forgiven" (Mark 4:11–12). But if Jesus desired anything in his ministry, it was that people should perceive and understand his message, turn, and be forgiven![7] He was no purveyor of esoteric doctrine, nor was Christianity simply another mystery religion like many of that day. Whatever mystery of the kingdom existed then—and the mystery still persists, else there would be fuller agreement on it—the purpose of Jesus was certainly to clarify and not to obscure his message.

With this understanding of the setting, the parables of growth are a natural part of the teaching of Jesus about the nature of the kingdom. With sure insight he linked aspiration with action in "Thy kingdom come. Thy will be done on earth." He doubtlessly foresaw and at times felt in his own labors frustration and discouragement, and the parables of growth were promises of hope. One might see little immediate fruit of one's labors, but if one sowed the seed with fidelity and waited in faith, God would give the increase.

Let us now look briefly at each of these parables separately. The point of the parable of the sower, if we may bypass the details of the allegorical explanation, is that the seed is the gospel being proclaimed by Jesus; the soil is the Christian who is called to witness to it and to live by its demands under many thwarting circumstances. Not all sowing will bear fruit, but some seed will fall on good ground and bring forth a rich harvest as the reward of faith and steadfastness. The harvest is the coming of the kingdom of God.[8]

The tares—or weeds from which we have made a verb out of the need of weeding them out—are the ever-present forces of evil. These are familiar enough to be consistent with any interpretation of the kingdom, whether apocalyptic, prophetic, realized eschatology, or existential decision. They stand for the evil forces enticing Christ's followers away from the gospel, the church, and the kingdom. We are not to suppose that Jesus was counseling his disciples to be indifferent to such evil or acquiescent in it; his entire ministry looks in the opposite direction.

What it probably means is that it is impossible to have a "pure" church and offenders should not be purged, their final judgment being left in the hands of God.

The mustard seed may not literally be the smallest of all seeds; this need not trouble us. The point of the parable is growth from small beginnings to great expansion. This hope of great things yet to come through God's action in spite of the world's resistant forces must have nourished Jesus himself when faced with opposition and apparent defeat, and it was a note greatly needed by his followers. It goes without saying, perhaps, that this has been a perennial and is still a contemporary need of Christians.

The leaven is paired with the mustard seed as an assurance of the growth of the church and the spread of the gospel through witness to and acceptance of God's kingly rule. When Paul and the rabbinical writers speak of leaven, they use it as a symbol for evil influences (I Cor. 5:6–8), and Jesus himself elsewhere warns his hearers to "beware of the leaven of the Pharisees" (Matt. 16:6; Luke 12:1), and in Mark, of Herod also (Mark 8:15). The use of leaven in the parable to describe the growth of the kingdom suggests that God's power transcends that of any countervailing force.

The parable of the earth bearing fruit of itself, or as is sometimes said, the seed growing secretly, has the same note of growth toward the harvest as do those of the sower, the tares, and the mustard seed. Yet a note that is implicit in the other parables of growth here becomes explicit. Growth indeed requires human effort; the seed has to be scattered on the ground. Yet the growing power is there in the creativity God has placed within it. Jesus appears to be saying that the kingdom will come in due course by God's action; his followers may wait in confidence that a power not their own is at work in the process.

This is not to suggest that Jesus spelled out, in a philosophical system, the thought of a divine energy at work in the world. It is certain that he did not, though the germ of it is there in his thinking of God as the Creator whose presence and care are manifest in even the smallest things of his creation. The parable is distorted if we try to read out of it a doctrine of inevitable progress; yet it is quite in keeping with the process theology of today which sees a forward movement through the tender and loving concern of a transcendent yet immanent God.

Obviously all five of these parables are designed to give encouragement and hope. But how do they bear on our present understanding of the kingdom of God?

In the earlier part of this century such sayings of Jesus were often cited to reinforce belief in an evolutionary progress toward a better world. This took various forms. The coming of the kingdom was conceived by some, though not by its major exponents, as a gradual growth in goodness on earth until it would finally fruit in a utopian perfection. Many who did not go this far stressed the need of human effort to build the kingdom, with a strong emphasis on the need to attack and eliminate the social evils of war, injustice, and oppression. For this reason it is often referred to as the social gospel kingdom.

I do not believe that this is what Jesus was saying when he spoke the parables of growth. Some now call them parables of contrast to avoid this interpretation. An evolutionary optimism leading eventually to a perfect society would have been inconceivable to Jesus, and if he could have conceived it he would have rejected it. His apocalyptic expectancy is in the background even where it is not so expressly stated as in the parables of the last judgment or the tares.

But does this mean that we must accept his apocalyptic imagery to find value in the parables? And does it mean that we are on false ground to stress human responsibility for the advancement of the kingdom? And does it cancel out a social gospel? The answer to all three of these crucial questions is an emphatic no!

If the reader has gone along with what has been said in the earlier chapters, Jesus was an apocalyptist in the currents of his time, but this never contradicted his main message of the love and saving power of God and the need to love and serve one's fellows in obedient response to the call of God. If this is accepted, it follows that the kingdom does not come automatically or even supernaturally, but it advances through the creativity of God as Christ's followers accept their responsibility as God's servants. Then, a social gospel in the form of the call to increase both love and justice in human society at manifold points is not only acceptable but imperative. Every one of the parables of growth then falls into place.

6. The parables of judgment

We come now to a group of parables in which Jesus' apocalypticism is more clearly evident than in those previously examined. Yet even here they say something to us that is of permanent worth and truth, whether or not we adopt their apocalyptic framework.

Let us first look briefly at some miscellaneous parables of judgment introduced by the words, "The kingdom of heaven is like. . ." There is, first, the parable of the dragnet (Matt. 13:47–50). All sorts of fish are gathered in. Jesus was never a purist as to those to whom the gospel should be preached, and the bad might be gathered with the good. Yet at the close of the age there will be divine separation. The reference to the furnace of fire and to men weeping and gnashing their teeth, which reappears in several of the subsequent parables of judgment, is straight out of Jewish eschatology. There is no certainty that Jesus used these words, in fact there is the probability that he did not. In any case, they are so at variance with his understanding of God as a loving Father that it is tragic that they have so often been taken literally.

We come next to the parable of the unforgiving servant (Matt. 18:23-35). This is also a parable of judgment, though its eschatological note appears only in the last sentence of it. Unlike the words just cited, this is fully in keeping with the words of the Lord's Prayer. God forgives without limit the penitent sinner; he asks that we forgive also those who wrong us. An unforgiving spirit merits divine judgment.

The parable of the great banquet, which in somewhat variant forms appears in Matthew 22:1-14 and Luke 14:12-24, has as its theme the divine invitation which must be accepted without excuses. The invited guests are left out of the feast by their self-centered preoccupation with lesser concerns; the poor, the maimed, the blind, the lame, those in the byways and hedges are sought out and welcomed. This may be a dig at the self-righteousness of the religious elite, and especially in its form in Luke it may be taken as a vindication of the mission to the Gentiles. Yet probably its primary note is the then familiar symbolism of the heavenly banquet and the modes of response to it. In this setting it is another way of putting the basic and initial call of Jesus, "Repent, for the kingdom of heaven is at hand."

We look now at a sequence in Matthew 24 and 25 where there is a vivid account of the end of the age and the troubles just preceding it. The parables of crisis here are those of the thief in the night (24:43-44); the faithful and unfaithful servants (24:45-51); the wise and foolish maidens (25:1-13); the talents (25:14-30); and the last judgment (25:31-46). Mark and Luke have also a parable of the waiting servants (Mark 13:33-37; Luke 12:35-46) which may be a variation of that of the faithful and unfaithful servants but is not identical with it. The note that is sounded in all these parables is the need of watchfulness and fidelity in view of the coming of the Son of man, yet the uncertainty of the hour in which this will occur.

The varieties of interpretation placed upon these parables epitomize the entire problem of the kingdom of God with which this book is concerned. C. H. Dodd from the angle of realized eschatology and his conviction that Jesus believed the kingdom had already come in his own person interprets them as originally spoken by Jesus to refer to the crisis connected with his own death and resurrection.[9] Others who believe that Jesus could not have said these things attribute them to the early church and the error of the evangelists in presenting them as his words. Those who believe that Jesus was an apocalyptist accept them in the main as authentic, but with wide variation as to whether we should expect from them a literal second coming. The ordinary Christian in one of the mainline churches, more inclined to look to the Bible for directions for living than concerned with problems of textual criticism, is apt to draw from them only an injunction to fidelity and perhaps a warning to be ready to die, since death may overtake one at any moment. If he is a member of one of the Pentecostal or Adventist churches, or a literalist in any of the others, the series of woes and warnings in Matthew 24 are a sure sign in our troubled time that we are living in the last days and Christ is coming soon.

The position which has been defended in this book is that Jesus was influenced by the apocalyptic expectations of his time and probably did speak some such words as these, expecting an imminent day of the Lord which did not occur. His followers, still expecting its occurrence, passed them on with their own interpretations. This does not detract from his divinity or uniqueness as the Son of God or as the Son of man, if we see in the latter term not a supernatural heavenly messenger, but the humanity which is essential to any true incarnation. Jesus was apocalyptic, but so much more than that that this element becomes wholly subordinate to his revelation of the nature and will of God. Thus his apocalypticism was unique in that it was suffused with moral and spiritual, and thus with prophetic, elements.

We see this blend of an apocalyptic framework with a prophetic message most clearly in the parable of the last judgment or the sheep and the goats. But it is evident in all the others. Let us now look at them in succession.

The parable of the thief coming in the night with the householder unprepared is a very brief one occupying only two verses and appears in nearly identical form in Matthew 24:43–44 and Luke 12:39–40. Since Paul uses the same figure of speech when he says in I Thessalonians 5:2, "For you yourselves know well that the day of the Lord will come like a thief in the night," we may conclude that this entered the thought of the church very early. In Matthew it is preceded by a section which sounds the note of preparedness by a backward look at the unpreparedness at the time of Noah and the flood and a forward-oriented prediction of the hour when two persons will be in the field or grinding at the mill, one taken and the other left. The setting in Luke ties it in with the reward of faithfulness given to the servants whom the master finds waiting for him when he comes home from the marriage feast.

The parable of the faithful and unfaithful servants is also found in both Matthew and Luke, directly after the reference to the thief at night (Matt. 24:45–51; Luke 12:41–48). In each case the story begins with the question, "Who then is the faithful and wise servant, whom his master has set over his household, to give them their food at the proper time?" It continues with the reward of the good and the punishment of the bad servant. But the endings differ. In both, the unfaithful servant is "cut in pieces" according to both KJV and the New English Bible with this as a marginal reading in the Revised Standard Version—a fate hardly consistent with the spirit and message of Jesus, and we are under no obligation to believe that he ever said it. Matthew follows this with his being put with the hypocrites; there men will weep and gnash their teeth—an obvious reference to hell. But Luke in a milder vein differentiates between those who know and those who do not know the master's will and ends with a great word in the best prophetic tradition, "Every one to whom much is given, of him will much be required" (12:48).

The parable of the ten maidens (Matt. 25:1-13) better known as the ten virgins, is the first of three longer parables in the sequence which Matthew provides, and it is found only in Matthew. Also, it is the only one of this group which is expressly introduced by a comparison with the kingdom of heaven, though all in this sequence are sufficiently in the same vein to indicate that to the writer, the coming of the Son of man, on the day of the Lord, was to be the coming of the kingdom.

The one point of the parable is the need of responsible alertness. There is no evidence of positive moral turpitude on the part of the foolish maidens: they were simply not wise enough and did not take pains enough to be ready. Nobody else could make amends for their negligence. No censure is placed on the bridegroom for keeping them waiting until midnight—it was their business to be prepared, and since they were not ready, the door was shut.

It is, of course, easy to turn this into a bit of simple counsel that one should always think ahead and be ready for emergencies. But to do this is to miss the point of the parable. The early church was waiting for the *parousia*. A good many years had gone by since the death of Jesus, and he had not yet returned. The church needed reassurance that he would still come in spite of the delay, and those becoming lax needed to be prodded.

They needed to know that nobody else could make the preparation for them, and there was no second chance beyond the "great day." This parable in its time served all these purposes.

As the point of the parable of the ten maidens is responsible alertness, so that of the talents is responsible use of what has been entrusted to us by God. The modern use of the word talent as a special gift or capacity is drawn directly from the biblical parable of the talents, where it meant a sum of money of about one thousand dollars, and in either case it should be viewed as something held in trust.

As Jesus originally spoke the parable, it may have had no eschatological flavor. But as Matthew has used it (25:14–30) and Luke in his similar parable of the pounds (19:11–27), it has taken on this connection. It need not trouble us that the man going on a journey is represented as a hard man driving a shrewd bargain for his own gain, for the parable does not focus on the character of God or of Christ. Its intent is to say that while waiting for the Master's return, Christians should be active, use their talents instead of hiding them, take risks, be about the Master's business.

There may also be a reference to the Jewish leaders, whether in Jesus' time or later, who viewed their function only as preserving the law rather than bringing about change. In any case, the current Jewish idea of Gehenna is evident in the end of the story with the injunction to "cast the worthless servant into the outer darkness; there men will weep and gnash their teeth." This, if nothing more, we may regard as Matthew's contribution to the story.

The climax of the series is found in the great picture of the last judgment. Here, as was noted earlier, the apocalyptic and prophetic notes are most fully blended. The setting is apocalyptic. The story begins with the great assize "when the Son of man comes in his glory," and it ends with the decisive verdict of assignment either to eternal punishment or to eternal life. But midway the mark of the kingdom is humaneness, loving service, a deep concern for human need. One's final destiny hinges on feeding the hungry, welcoming the stranger, clothing the destitute, caring for the sick, showing solicitude for the prisoner. In different words, but with the same spirit, there is reflected here the message which Jesus took from the prophet Isaiah and made the keynote of his ministry, "The Spirit of the Lord God is upon me, because the Lord has anointed me to bring good tidings to the afflicted" (Isa. 61:1). Furthermore, it is in keeping with his conception of his own messiahship, or at least of a special vocation from God, as he states it in response to a query of John the Baptist, "Are you he who is to come, or shall we look for another?" The reply he gives is, "Go and tell John what you hear and see: the blind receive their sight and the lame walk, lepers are cleansed and the deaf hear, and the dead are raised up, and the poor have good news preached to them" (Matt.11:3–5).

These parables of judgment enunciate a very important aspect of the message of Jesus and of Christian faith as a whole —namely the reality of judgment as well as mercy in the nature of God and the nature of the kingdom. But what kind of judgment, and how does it come upon the sinner? This still looms as a large question to which some attention will be given in later chapters.

We cannot here give special attention to each of the parables of Jesus. But enough has been said to indicate their trend and various essential aspects of the kingdom in the mind of Jesus. Altered though these stories doubtlessly were during the years between the time when Jesus spoke and the evangelists wrote them, the message is still discernible. From them we glean what has previously been indicated as basic notes in the understanding of the kingdom: the timeless kingship, or kingly rule, of God; an ongoing and present kingdom to be entered and lived in by accepting God's sovereign rule in obedient response; and a final victory of God which is in God's hands, though he calls us to labor in faith and love for its coming. Thus, the kingdom is both presence and promise; both within and beyond human history; God's gift and man's task; we work for it, even as we wait for it.

VI
The Difference It Makes

We have now concluded a survey of the biblical sources most relevant to a resolution of the dilemma regarding the kingdom of God which was outlined in the first chapter. We have looked at the types of understanding of the kingdom most influential in the twentieth century; at the position which this author holds to be most acceptable; at the ideological framework of the times within which Jesus spoke and the evangelists later wrote; and in particular at the parables as giving our clearest evidence of the mind of Christ upon this matter. There is much more that could be said, but this is perhaps enough to provide a sufficient theological and biblical foundation for making up one's mind on the issue. Without some such foundation and searching the Scriptures, one jumps too easily at a conclusion somewhere along the wide spectrum of opinion. Or, one decides no problem is involved, and there is no use of stirring up the question. Or one may simply bypass it as too controversial or insoluble.

The purpose of this chapter is to try to indicate that what one thinks about the central message of Jesus matters greatly, not only as an academic question of biblical interpretation and a theological quest for truth, but as a matter of personal and social living. What Christians think, or perhaps more often assume as unexamined attitudes, has much to do with what Christians do—or fail to do. And what Christians do or fail to do is both the product of the churches' efforts and the seedbed for their future effectiveness in today's world.

The Difference It Makes

1. The world we live in

As a backdrop for discussing the bearing of the kingdom of God on personal living, social action, the state of the churches today, and their possible service to the future, let us assemble some familiar facts about our present world. This survey need not be extensive and may not say anything not already known to the reader, but the facts need to be assembled for a composite view. They contain some alarming items, and we need to retain our perspective. I am not by nature a pessimist, and I do not believe that everything is wrong with our world. In another context I might include a chapter on "What Is Right with Modern Life" as I did some years ago in *The Modern Rival of Christian Faith,* and most of the things there mentioned are still here and still right.[1] But along with the good things and some advances over the past years, there is too much that is wrong.

Let us begin with a development that has had both good and bad effects on modern life and has affected radically the lives of all of us. First, then, this is a world of brilliant scientific and technological achievement. It is a world undreamed of at the beginning of this century, and due to great medical advances which are a part of it, a good many of us are still living whose memories span this entire century. It is one of the rewards of growing older that one can recall seeing these things happen! To mention a few of them: the coming of the radio and more recently the television; the cinema,—first silent, then talking, then colored; quick and easy communication by telephone, an accepted part of life—first to one's neighbors, then across the continent, then to the other side of the earth, then to a space ship, and to the moon. Add to these the conquest of space by the airplane as the normal mode of long distance travel, and the automobile which began to be used before the turn of the century has become so much a part of life to millions that a curtailment of gasoline sends the economy into a tailspin. Then add to these

117

the computer with a host of other advances in electronics, and the nuclear space age as a whole, and we have a vast structure of modern miracles. Yet, we have become so much accustomed to these man-made miracles, that we do not marvel at them much any more. The miracles in the Bible we may still puzzle over, to accept, reject, or try to explain, but the miracles around us we do not think much about except to make use of them.

In the second place, we live in a very dangerous world. Some of these dangers stem directly from the brilliant achievements that have just been outlined. There are dangers not only from death on the highways and in the air, but from the wide-spread pollution and destruction of the environment which have made ecology an important concern and at many points a challenge to technology. Nuclear fission, one of the most brilliant of these achievements, has introduced the fear of atomic destruction, perhaps to be world wide, and has increased the arms race under the aegis of national security and with it an enormous expenditure of military funds which might otherwise be available for domestic services. Yet so prone are we to care most about what is near at hand, the fear of atomic destruction is probably less keen in most minds than is the energy crisis which means less oil and gasoline available, less fuel for heating, and an abrupt change in American life-styles. Steadily rising prices, the danger of continuing inflation, an economic recession as bad or worse than the Great Depression of the early 1930s, and widespread unemployment that can hit almost anywhere give plenty to worry about.

In between these dangers, whether remote or close at hand, lies overpopulation, the maldistribution of the natural resources of the world including food, and as a result the malnutrition of over half—some say two-thirds—of the world's population. While better agriculture increases the available food, the population increases faster. There are too many people, as in the southward-moving Sahara Desert, who are now starving, and many others are so undernourished as to be not far from the edge of starvation. With the present population of about three and a half billion people expected to increase to twice that number by the end of the century, and unless halted to increase by geometric ratio beyond that point, this alone would justify saying that we live in a dangerous world.

In the third place, it is a world of startling social and personal immorality. This statement needs to be guarded for two reasons. One is that there are many thousands—probably many millions in the aggregate—of decent, kind, honest people in the world who by any ordinary standards could be considered moral. The second is that these same people, or at least many of us, are apt to deplore with shock the overt immorality of others without looking within at our own less conspicuous, but self-satisfied, immoral attitudes. Yet allowing for wholesome exceptions and also for the fact that there are inevitable differences of opinion as to what is considered immoral, we can still say that ours is a time of startling immorality.

To try to state briefly the vast range of evidences along this line is probably futile, but the attempt must be made. There is a world-wide oppression of the exploited for personal gain, whether in material goods or control or often both. There is repression or rejection of persons and denial of opportunities through race, sex, and other forms of prejudice. We are shocked to learn of corruption in high places in government. Cheating of one kind or another, dishonesty, and lying as an attempted cover-up are widely accepted practices in many fields. Defiance of the sex standards of the ages, both in personal relations and in the mores of the entertainment world, is justified in the name of freedom. People defile their own or others' bodies with ruinous drugs, which include alcohol which is socially accepted as well as marijuana, LSD, or heroin which drinking parents deplore when their children use them.

Mixed in with all this is an increase in crime and violence. Yet outside the circles of overt crime, and found in many "good" people, is justification of the violence of war and condemnation of those young persons whose consciences will not let them participate in it. And among those many persons who have committed no illegal act of crime or of overt violence, there is a widespread self-centeredness and demand for the right to do what one pleases which results in the violence of serious hurt to others. Add to this the structural violence built into the social system, and the scene looks dark.

Some of the forms of immorality thus outlined are clearly contrary to the time-honored, yet still relevant, Ten Commandments. Some may be somewhat in limbo because of differing opinions as to what is right, for example, abortion which is regarded by some as horribly immoral and by others as a legitimate step in some cases toward better family life with better rearing of those children who are born, and toward a better-fed world. But permeating most of the issues which have been surveyed is sin in the sense of violation of the Hebrew-Christian love commandment and an indifference to the call of God for moral responsibility in all of life. And where there is sin, God's judgment is real.

Fourth, it is a very dissatisfied world. On the one hand, there is much oppression and lack of the freedoms of thought, speech, action, livelihood, and self-fulfillment at its best which every person, in the dignity of personhood, ought to have. On the other hand, there are many freedoms, lauded even by some psychiatrists, which are sought and claimed in indifference to the rights and freedoms of others, and which end, not in true self-fulfillment, but in an egocentric self-seeking and self-pity in the frustration of these desires. Much pleasure is sought and there are manifold forms of entertainment to provide it, but the pleasure is apt to prove tasteless and transient. Some deeper forms of disturbance, such as deep disappointments, sickness, bereavement and death, are perennial. Yet others are the result of our too complex and high-tensioned society. Clashes within the family or the work situation that cause resentment, hard feelings and then severance; anonymity and rootlessness in an overcrowded but lonely world; uncertainty as to the future and even as to whether there will be a future—these elements in our society rob many of what ought to be the rich satisfactions of living.

What this all adds up to is an unsettled and anxious, even at points despairing, world. This is not to suggest that there are no happy people in it, for there are. I do not wish to be among the harbingers of doom who speak and write frequently in these days as if there were nothing good to be said. It is possible to point to very significant advances within the past century, both here and in other nations. In spite of much that still needs to be done, we had better rejoice and be thankful, not only for more comfortable living with the vast range of things technology has produced, but for more recognition of race and sex equality and advances toward implementation of these principles; better education; better health; minimum wage, unemployment and social security provisions; and a large network of social agencies that we sometimes fume at as being bureaucratic and expensive but which few of us would want to see abolished. In the churches we may add a greater ecumenical understanding and fellowship, a greater outreach in service to society, and an effort, however varied in its success, at inner renewal.

These factors should keep us from falling into despair. Yet this is an uneasy time and for great numbers of people, their morale is low. They lack both firm rootage for living in the present and hope for the future. At this point, whether in good circumstances or bad, Christian faith and especially that aspect of it which Jesus called the kingdom of God, becomes highly relevant.

2. Types of response

How have the people responded to these circumstances? And especially the church people? The responses have varied, and it is impossible to set forth categories in which to pigeonhole individuals or groups within precise limits. Yet general trends can be observed, and some indication can be given as to the relation of these trends to the theme of this book.

The secular public has for the most part deplored these circumstances, looked for a scapegoat to take the blame, and found it in those in political or economic power. "Politics is rotten." "Big business" or "the unions," depending on which side of the economic terrain one is on, is responsible for the woes of the other side. Yet one feels that there is little one can do about it except try to keep going and make the best of it. The more action-minded engage in strikes, boycotts, and other forms of protest, with occasional outbreaks of violence. Yet for the most part there is still a feeling of helplessness and sullen rebellion. But if things are bad and can't be set right, let us enjoy ourselves any way we can! Pessimism, stoicism, and hedonism meet in an outlook that has few if any goals for the future, and in such as there are, only short-range ones.

Among those comfortably situated, things may not seem so bad. Life has not only comforts but personal satisfactions, and things are going to be better after awhile. Still, one is not too sure, for the stock market goes up and down very uncertainly. For large numbers, it is impossible to have even this much assurance. For the poor, the unemployed, and those facing the stark possibility of unemployment, the future looks very dark.

Amid this widespread feeling of helplessness and an ensuing

apathy and anxiety, the churches are little trusted if not rejected outright. They are thought not to have the leverage or the expertise in major social issues to make much difference, and are often condemned for an apparent indifference to such matters. For help in personal problems one goes to a psychiatrist or perhaps to a marriage counselor if one can afford it. If not, one muddles along as best one can.

In such a situation the eschatological question, "What is the world coming to?" is often asked. It seldom receives an eschatological answer from the general public or mainline churches. It would be a quite unusual occurrence if one were to bring the current social situation into close connection with the kingdom of God. But the adventists do this, as we shall see presently. Before examining how they do it, let us look at the situation in the mainline churches.

3. In the mainline churches

The well-established churches with a long heritage and social recognition are designated as mainline to distinguish them from the sects, which have proliferated enormously in America. The sects have broken away from the main stream over some issue that they regard as wrongly or too meagerly stressed by the parent church. It should not be regarded as a pejorative term, for the sects sometimes develop into mainline churches, as did the early Methodists. Each sect needs to be judged on its own merits.

In the mainline churches as elsewhere, the response to the current situation is somewhat varied. Yet a widely prevalent aspect of the variation is polarization within the membership. This is conspicuous at a number of points.

A form of polarization of long standing is theological with biblical interpretation as its center. In most of the denominations there is still a considerable number of biblical literalists (self-styled conservatives but called fundamentalists by others) who refuse to accept the views of modern historical and textual scholarship as to the true meanings of the Bible. The liberals seem to them to be subverting the gospel, while the liberals view the fundamentalists as retarding the advance of knowledge and obscuring a wealth of meaning in the Scriptures. What one thinks about the kingdom of God depends in no small measure on this issue.

This line of separation has become less acute than it was fifty years ago when the famous Dayton trial over the right to teach evolution in the public schools took place, and in the same year of 1925 Harry Emerson Fosdick had to leave the pastorate of the First Presbyterian Church of New York City because of his theological views. The literalist point of view is now more common among the sects than in the mainline churches, but it still has its adherents in the latter, as any denominational paper which has a forum of letters to the editor will make evident.

A related but not identical form of polarization is between the exponents of social action as a necessary form of Christian witness and those who would keep the churches only to the sphere of personal religion. This is a deeper and more serious division than the theological one. Conservatives in one of these areas are apt to be so in the other, but not always. A call for the elimination of exploitation of the weak by the strong, of racial and other forms of discrimination, of corruption in business and government, of poverty and its causes, and of the giant evil of war is an offshoot of the earlier social gospel, though not identical with it. The difference lies mainly in the fact that the earlier exponents of the social gospel thought of the coming of the kingdom of God as progressive growth toward a better world through the conquest of these social evils. However, this identification is less often made today, though the former tensions are still present. The denominational leaders and seminary-trained clergy are apt to believe that a prophetic social witness as well as ministry to personal life are essential aspects of the churches' mission. Large segments of the laity, more prone to think as the environing culture does, disapprove this approach.

This unfortunate cleavage is said to be deeper in America than in the churches of any other part of the world.[2] Since the full gospel, like a full understanding of the kingdom, requires both love and justice and an extension of love and justice from the mind and heart of the individual Christian to the world, this polarization is a serious barrier to the service of the churches. It provides more than a little of the reason why so many ministers, especially among the recent seminary graduates, prefer some kind of social or educational ministry to service in the local parish.

Other types of polarization in the churches are less acute and may be mentioned more briefly. One of these has to do with modes of ministry to the personal life. The clergy today are better trained in pastoral care than ever before, and most of them take this responsibility seriously. Yet their psychological training tends to accent self-acceptance and to minimize sin, and this makes for an approach which subordinates a basic aspect of the message of Jesus—his call to penitence. "Repent, for the kingdom of heaven is at hand" sounds archaic to modern ears.

Another form of polarization has to do with evangelism. Many if not most Christian leaders believe that evangelism in the sense of a call to Christian commitment is an essential part of Christian witness. One may rejoice that evangelism is not the bad word it was for a long time in many of the mainline churches. But, evangelism in what form? Here the cleavage appears. Some strongly support the efforts of Billy Graham, of the Campus Crusade for Christ, or other such mass appeals. Others believe that the Christian witness is borne best in the ongoing work of the churches and through small groups, re-treats, or other gatherings directed toward personal growth in the Christian life.

Still another form of polarization which has recently swung into prominence is centered in the charismatic movement. At its best, this movement accents the reality and the work of the Holy Spirit—God present with us for guidance, for comfort, and for strength—which is basic to any true or effective Christian experience. But the movement does not stop at this point. In some forms it so stresses the baptism of the Spirit as a gift granted to some but withheld from others that it easily runs into a "holier than thou" attitude which imperils the basic virtue of Christian humility. Again, it encourages speaking in tongues as the chief expression and even as the only evidence of the baptism of the Spirit. When it takes these turns, it is inevitably divisive.

The last form of polarization to which I shall call attention is in regard to forms of corporate worship. In the movement toward the renewal of the church and from the desire to make the churches relevant to the modern age, a good many innovative services have been introduced. Along with these, and apparently from a desire to accent the joyous rather than the austere aspects of Christian worship, celebration has become customary. When these newer forms of worship have reverence, dignity, and fitness, and when it is the greatness and glory of God that is celebrated rather than the worshiper's own exuberance, there is much to commend them. Too often these requirements are not met and under the guise of worship they become forms of lively entertainment, perhaps appropriate elsewhere but hardly so in the sanctuary of a church. Confession of sin or a call to penitence is rarely expressed. Informality reigns. Polarization emerges between the exponents of novelty and those who wish to retain at least the central aspects of traditional worship.

What shall we do about these divisions? It is obvious that the churches are weakened when some members withdraw or with-hold their moral and financial support because they do not like what is being done or said by others. On the other hand, we cannot force everybody into one mold. In a pluralistic society of which the churches are a part, we cannot expect all to think alike, and the very fact that the thinking is in religious terms gives it a force it might not otherwise have. Dogmatism, like despotism, is unhealthy wherever it appears. But so are divisions of opinion which breed personal animosities and weaken what should be the shared witness of the Christian gospel. Can we not find a cause great enough to bring us together across the gaps?

This could be found in a renewed devotion to the kingdom of God. In all of this social and religious upheaval, where is our concern for the kingdom? There is general agreement that it was the central message of Jesus. Why is it not central today? In the conventional forms of worship, the Lord's Prayer is still said. Other than that, one could attend a good many services of Christian worship without hearing the kingdom mentioned. Basic elements are there in both social and personal religion, but the connection is seldom spelled out. Further attention to this theme with its bearing on the problems of our life together might make for better living and for stronger churches.

4. In the adventist sects

How fares the kingdom of God in the adventists sects? There are too many of these to discuss in any detail. Furthermore, adventism is not limited to the sects, but is found in the conservative churches and the fundamentalist corps of the mainline churches. It is based on a literalist interpretation of the apocalyptic literature of the Bible, particularly that of Daniel and Revelation, in which various texts and passages are quoted as containing hidden or overt meanings and prophecies which validate belief in an anticipated second coming of Christ in our time, and with it the coming of the kingdom of God. The apocalyptic sayings of Jesus are much quoted, but others are cited to establish the time as being in the very near future. In general, the thought centers in a cosmic conflict between God and Satan, with the world having become so corrupt that only divine intervention to end the present regime and usher in a new one will avail to change it. There is, accordingly, little trust in human social action, but great confidence that human ills can be corrected for the faithful by the bliss that will follow the cataclysmic, yet glorious, coming of the kingdom of God.

The best known and the largest of these groups are the Seventh Day Adventists and the Jehovah's Witnesses. The former, an outgrowth of the zeal of William Miller in the 1840s, may now be considered more as a church than a sect. It carries on mission work in most of the countries of the world, has hospitals, colleges, and other schools in many lands, and has done much for the amelioration of human suffering as well as for the propagation of its faith. It is hardly typical of the usual adventist position. Jehovah's Witnesses are a clearer example and will be discussed further. There are too many forms of adventism to examine all of them in any detail.

It is not difficult to discover what the Jehovah's Witnesses believe, for their faithful witnesses—usually neatly dressed young people—come frequently to our doors distributing the periodicals *Awake!* and *The Watchtower* and seeking the opportunity to come in and give a Bible lesson. I have a number of copies of these before me as I write. *Awake!* is said by its publishers to be the most widely read news magazine in the world, published in 29 languages in more than 200 countries with 7,500,000 copies of each issue.[3] During 1973, 41 "Divine Victory" assemblies were held in 38 cities of the world, with many thousands often in attendance and a total of 39,313 baptisms of new members. The contemporary influence of the Jehovah's Witnesses is not to be taken lightly!

But what do we observe from this literature? First, take a look at a four-page brochure distributed by the millions. It is entitled, "Is Time Running Out For Mankind?" Two pages present evidence that the answer is yes. World wars, massive famines, disease epidemics, violent crimes, and global pollution increasing since 1914 mark that year as the beginning of the last days foretold by Bible prophecy. On the fourth page is the arresting caption, which could cause one to shudder but is designed to induce rejoicing, "You can be happy that so little time is left." This statement is defended by the promise to "honest-hearted" persons that with the coming of God's kingdom in the near future there will be lasting peace, eternal life without sickness, no more crime and hunger, and the earth will be a delightful home.[4]

This in essence is adventist belief, though elaborated elsewhere with accounts of the anticipated divine victory in the last great battle with Satan at Armageddon. But why 1914 as the beginning of the last days? And why this generation? Social changes for the worse are stated to corroborate the woes predicted in Matthew 24:7–29, Mark 13:6–24, and Luke 21:10–26. But the chronology is determined by an ingenious use of other Bible passages. The year 607 B.C. is taken as the date of the fall of Jerusalem to the forces of Nebuchadnezzar, though modern scholarship places this event in 587 B.C. In Revelation 12:6 the woman who had borne a male child that would rule all nations fled into the wilderness and was nourished there for 1,260 days. Again in verse 14 she is referred to as being nourished "for a time, and times, and half a time." What the author was probably referring to in these cryptic words is divine protection of the persecuted church in the last decade of the first century when the book was written to sustain the faithful. What the Jehovah's

Witnesses do with it is to take "a time" to mean a year, and add these periods of 1,260 days and three and a half years to make seven years, or 2,520 days. In Numbers 14:34 and Ezekiel 4:5, 6 God's punishment is meted out on the basis of "a day for each year." Count the time from 607 B.C. to A.D. 1914, called the Gentile Times, and it comes close to 2,520 years!

But how are we to understand the word of Jesus, "Truly, I say to you, this generation will not pass away till all these things take place" (Matt. 24:34)? The answer is that those who were living in 1914 are dead or getting old and cannot live much longer. The second coming will occur before this generation ends.[5]

A more erudite presentation of adventism is found in a book that has had an enormous sale since its publication in 1970, Hal Lindsey's *The Late Great Planet Earth.*[6] Many passages are cited from the Bible, regardless of their historic setting and context, as prophecies that the end of the world is coming soon. The author makes much of the seven years of Revelation 11:2, 3 as a countdown period, or time of tribulations, which will inaugurate the end. But instead of 1914, it is the return of the Jews to their homeland that is the signal, and this generation begins in 1948. There they will rebuild the temple and turn in large numbers to Christ. There they will be assailed, and the last great battle will take place, and current events are leading up to it. Russia is Gog of the land of Magog. Egypt will suffer the terrible fate predicted by Isaiah in chapter 19. Japan and China are the kings of the East that imperil the world. The successor of Rome as the beast with ten horns of Daniel 7 is the European Common Market, and from this revived Roman Empire a future führer will emerge as Antichrist. The great harlot, Babylon, of Revelation 17 who will subvert the people is "one world religion," apostate and ecumenical, to which are added the idolatries of astrology, witchcraft, and drugs.

But what of the end? The author has it in two stages. The first will be the rapture, or translation—he calls it "the ultimate trip"—at the beginning of the seven years when many believers are suddenly caught up to meet Christ in the air. Then after Armageddon will come the Messiah, physically and visibly through the heavens to Mount Moriah from which he ascended, accompanied by "clouds of witnesses" in white robes returning in their immortal glorified bodies. "Perhaps the 'sign of the Son of man' will be a gigantic celestial image of Jesus flashed upon the heavens for all to see. This would explain how all men suddenly recognize who He is and see the scars from His piercing at the cross." [7]

The reader is entitled to make what he will of this. Apparently many accept it. I for one believe that such a presentation is no service to one who desires to understand the great truths of the Bible or find firm foundations for his Christian faith. I believe, as do the adventists, that there is great need of commitment to Christ and a personal religion that will give hope in troubled times and withstand the evil, even demonic, forces abroad in our world. I believe that the future victory of God is basic to the meaning of the kingdom of God. But there must be another way to conceive these great verities.

5. Some other conceptions

Such literalism and fantastic imagery is not the only way to think of Christ's return and the coming of the kingdom. Those readers who remember the Second Assembly of the World Council of Churches held in Evanston, Illinois, in 1954—the only one held thus far in the United States—will recall the long debate which preceded it over the main theme, "Jesus Christ, the hope of the world." When this was chosen as its theme, most Americans apparently assumed that this was intended to accent the hope that Jesus, the center of Christian faith, could bring to a deeply divided and troubled world. An Advisory Commission of scholars of international standing, a few from America but more from Europe and two from the Orient, was chosen to trace out the theme's implications. When they issued their first report, many Americans were dismayed to find a central emphasis given to the future return of Christ in glory—an understanding of the Christian hope long since relegated to the sects. The discussion this aroused led the Commission in their second report to distinguish between biblical eschatology and crude apocalypticism, to give more attention to the risen and living Christ in the individual Christian person, and to point out the bearings of Christian hope as a stimulus to action in contemporary society. Yet the return of Christ was still affirmed, with a neat balance between being "in Christ" and "expecting Christ." So it remained in the third and final statement, but with a more extended, vital, and moving affirmation of the kingdom that now is, of having and hoping, and of the kingdom that is to come. Many, including myself, found agreement easier than with the preceding presentations.

In the form in which this coming kingdom was eventually delineated, as divine victory and the final consummation of Christ's work on earth in both judgment and mercy, the biblical symbolism of Christ's return becomes meaningful. The Commission refused completely to make any estimate of the time when this would take place, declaring that "when we attempt to calculate the nearness or the distance of His Kingdom we confuse that hope of which Jesus Himself provides the clear pattern. His whole concern was the fulfilment of God's purpose rather than the satisfaction of man's curiosity." As to the character of the kingdom that is to come, the Commission said, "We must here speak of matters which, in the nature of things, defy direct expression in explicit speech, matters for which the language of inspired imagination employed in the Scriptures is alone adequate, for these are things that can be discerned and communicated only by the Spirit.'' Several examples of this inspired imagination are cited. The pure in heart shall see God. Those who are now sons of God will receive the fullness of their inheritance as joint heirs with Christ. There will be a new heaven and a new earth. The dead will be raised incorruptible, receiving a body of heavenly glory. Blind eyes will see; deaf ears will hear; the lame will leap for joy; the captive will be freed. The knowledge of God will cover the earth. The Holy City will appear, made ready as a bride adorned for her husband. The choir which no man can number will sing hallelujahs to the praise of the Eternal. All created things will be reconciled in the perfect communion of God with his people. ''It is in such visions as these that the Spirit enables us to point to the splendor of the salvation that is ready to be revealed in the last days. It is towards this salvation that God guides us in hope. This hope is not seen, or it would not be hope; but it is promised to us as suffering, sinning, dying, and believing men. Therefore we wait for it with patience.'' [8]

In the Assembly itself, not a great deal of reference was made to what had been wrought out so carefully after a three-year period of discussion. Yet some Americans in the mainline churches were emboldened by it to begin to speak about Christ's second coming. As far as I have been able to observe, this mood has not lasted to any great extent. Part of the reason is that interest in the main theme and its formulation passed as the Assembly itself passed into history. Another reason is that in America, the second coming is so deeply embedded in apocalyptic literalism, with its pessimism about the present world and hopelessness about any action to improve it, that any affirmation about Christ's return is bound to be identified with it. If one cannot affirm it to be understood on a deeper level, it may be better not to speak of a second coming but to accent Christ's living and continuing presence.

A further factor is that concern about Christian hope has shifted among scholars and those reading their books to another angle—tangent to the kingdom of God but not directly centered in it. This goes by the general caption of the theology of hope. But besides the illuminating *Theology of Hope* by Jürgen Moltmann[9] which introduced this trend in the 1960s, there are earlier but still recent trends which have claimed much attention: the process theology which looks to Alfred North Whitehead as its mentor and the evolutionary theology of Teilhard de Chardin, with Christ as the Omega Point towards which the whole creation moves. Of late we have heard much of the theology of liberation. Interest in these approaches to the future is not inconsistent with concern about the kingdom of God, but neither are they directly focused on it. This may be the reason why less writing has been done on the kingdom in the past twenty years than was formerly the case.

It would not be appropriate for me at this point to go into detail about these developments—had I the competence—for each would require a book in itself, or at best a chapter, to do it justice. I have absorbed helpful insights from each of them, but must now try to say something of how the kingdom of God as I understand it might make a difference in the world and the churches of today.

6. Hope, demand, and victory

The kingdom of God is both hope and demand, both promise and duty. If either element is left out, it fails to be what our biblical faith affirms it to be.

Said Paul, "We are saved by hope" (Rom. 8:24 KJV). The RSV makes it more explicit, "For in *this* hope we were saved" (italics mine). Everybody needs hope to keep going effectively in the daily demands of living, for without it motivation, energy, and action bog down. But more undergirding and uplifting than any other is the hope that comes to us in the message of Christ, the hope of the kingdom of God.

Not as a matter of theory only but of practical application, this hope is what our present distraught, endangered, and morally unstable world needs most. An ancient seer said it in words that never wear out, "Where there is no vision the people perish" (Prov. 29:18 KJV). Again the RSV gives it a somewhat different turn, equally applicable to our age, "Where there is no prophecy the people cast off restraint." Our society is largely without vision, which means without clear and adequate goals, and the result is rootlessness and instability. And there seems to be a dearth of prophets to point the way and inspire the vision. The vision both for personal living and a better society is to be found in the kingdom of God, provided we have the faith and the wisdom to find it.

But hope is not all we need. Look again at what we found in surveying the parables of Jesus, and in every one of them is a demand. We need to sense the supreme worth of the kingdom, which in other words means the supreme worth of love which is the essence of the kingdom's demands. We need to meet the conditions of entrance into the kingdom, of which penitence, humility, and trust are primary. Life in the kingdom is a life of obedience to God and of service in love to God and to one another. The parables of growth are promises of fruitage given by God, but also injunctions to fidelity. The parables of judgment tell us something we ought never to forget—that the righteous God of goodness and love demands righteousness of his people, and we cannot sin with impunity.

If such hope is available and such demands are to be taken seriously, the churches have a message worth proclaiming—one about which they ought never be silent. Hope is given us through the grace of God with divine forgiveness and the purging and strengthening of the inner life. But social action to "proclaim release to the captives and recovering of sight to the blind, to set at liberty those who are oppressed," we must certainly engage in. We must engage in it with a hope grounded in more than our human efforts and a response of the whole person to the call of God as the Holy Spirit shows us the way. Such a sense of mission may not eliminate all the forms of polarization in the churches, but it can go far toward bringing us to a greater unity and a more fruitful service to God and a needy world.

But how do the hope and the demands of the kingdom meet? And, once more, what is the kingdom of God? We found earlier that the three basic meanings drawn from the message of Jesus are God's universal and eternal kingly rule, the kingdom as an experience in personal life with obligations of service in love, and the kingdom as God's ultimate victory over evil in the final fulfilment of his purposes. Let us look a little further at each of these.

Without the sovereign, kingly rule of God over his world there would be no kingdom. In our day, when not many kings are left in the political orbit, the force of this term has tended to recede. But if we recognize that a king does not have to be a despot ruling tyrannically, kingly rule still has appropriate meaning. It means power, stability, a center of unity, a bulwark to the nation and hence to the people within it. The people of Jesus' time wanted a king like David to throw off the oppressor; Jesus taught them to put their trust in a different kind of king. In its most elemental meaning the kingdom of God means kingship, the just, righteous, and loving rule of God over his world.

But rule implies power. Can power and goodness meet in the God of Christian faith? This is an age-old question brought sharply to the fore by the tragic elements in modern life. We hear much of "the silence of God," and Jacques Ellul, a distinguished French lay theologian, has written a book entitled *Hope in Time of Abandonment* in which he presents evidence from the state of society and the church that God seems at least temporarily to have turned his back on the world.[10] Others hold that it is against the claims of reason to believe in the personal God of supreme love and power such as Jesus worshiped and served. This mood has had its effect in theology, and while few theologians go so far as to accept the death-of-God position, there is a movement away from a transcendent God of kingly power to an immanent spirit or process moving in man and the natural world.

There is some ground for these positions. In particular, the process theology, which conceives of God as working in tenderness and love to overcome the recalcitrant elements of evil and advance the world process by a continuous creation, is consistent with basic notes in Christian faith. Yet there is no adequate substitute for the New Testament understanding of God as both Creator and Redeemer, ruling his world in both power and love, offering to mankind both judgment and mercy, and affording a ground of security and hope for both present and future, for this world and for an ongoing life after death. The problem of evil is indeed serious, and I have indicated my views on this question in conjunction with the providence of God in another book.[11] This is not the place to go into it at length. Yet a brief summary of my position may be in order.

Turning to atheism because of the world's evil is no solution to the problem; for we are then left without explanation of the mystery of the good and the marvel of the intricate order and harmony of the world of nature. Asked to "count your many blessings, name them one by one" as the old hymn puts it, most people could find things to be thankful for—events, circumstances, persons—experiences that have yielded happiness. If systematized these would fall into three main types: the beauty, sustenance, and orderliness of nature on which our lives depend; social relations in the family, community, nation, and all our past which have nourished and fashioned us; and, less obviously but essentially, the human capacity of thought, feeling, and will by which to live and act as morally responsible beings.

These are gifts of the Creator. It is these relationships which give us security and happiness; it is these which can also cause suffering and, in the misuse of our freedom, sinning also. The one possibility necessitates the other. Then the suffering and sinning of individuals and groups cause it in others, for as the Bible puts it we are "bound in the bundle of life" (I Sam. 25:29).

We are not to suppose that God wills suffering and sin, and there is much pain which is not the result of sin. Yet there is suffering which is incurred as a result of defiance of the laws of God imbedded in the structure of the world, for there is both a physical and a moral order which cannot be trifled with. This is one form of the judgments of God. Another is the inner deterioration of personality that results from persistent self-centeredness and sinning. Both are very prevalent in our time. But though judgment and mercy are two sides of the divine rulership, it is not the will of God that pain and sin persist. We are called to work with him for their elimination.

Most of the world's evil is caused by the misuse of human freedom, either overtly or through indifference. We ought, therefore, not to say that God causes it. But why does not God intervene to stop it? Not through divine weakness, but through his self-limitation in having chosen to make a world with the great boons that have been indicated. We are to be God's servants in the eradication of its evils.

This we know by faith and the experience of the ages, that

God cares about our sin and suffering, seeks to redeem us from it, and whatever our plight, God will see us through if we will give him the opportunity. God never abandons us, though we may abandon him. Doubtlessly many readers can recall, as I do, dark experiences which we would not have chosen, but from which God has taught us much.

The High and Holy One who is vastly more than ourselves is also intimately near and ever moving within his world to sustain it and ourselves. This is the essence of the hope engendered by the rulership of the God who is both Creator and Redeemer. Nowhere have I seen this better stated than in the closing words of a great book, *God's Grace and Man's Hope,* by a great Christian and theologian, Daniel Day Williams. These words speak to me:

There is no situation in which the Christian cannot find meaning and hope. There is no social wrong which need remain unattacked, unmitigated, unreformed. There is no private desperate struggle with anxiety and bitterness and failure which cannot yield new hope when we discover that God does not leave us forsaken. But those who know this, while they are released to spend themselves in doing what needs to be done, live with a certain divine carelessness concerning earthly fortunes. Their hope sees beyond the years and they live in this demanding present under the everlasting assurance of God's love.[12]

God's rule is universal and timeless, and "though the wrong seems oft so strong, God is the ruler yet." But what of the kingdom in the present, among us here and now? I do not find the phrase "to enter the kingdom" being used much these days, discussion of the kingdom being centered mainly on the future when such discussion is carried on. Yet there is good biblical justification for such a present reference, and much meaning in it.

It is not necessary to accept in full the position of "realized eschatology" to believe that Jesus felt himself to have a special mission from God in ushering in the kingdom, and, furthermore, that the kingdom was present in and among his followers. There are numerous passages to support both of these conclusions, or a blend of the two. "The kingdom of God is upon you; repent, and believe the Gospel" (Mark 1:15 NEB). After the citation in the Nazareth synagogue of the words of Isaiah which Jesus took as defining his mission, "Today this scripture has been fulfilled in your hearing" (Luke 4:21). "But if it is by the Spirit of God that I cast out demons, then the kingdom of God has come upon you" (Matt. 12:28). Luke puts this more graphically, "by the finger of God" (Luke 11:20.)

The most crucial of all these passages is the briefest, "The kingdom of God is in the midst of you" (Luke 17:21). It is often said that the KJV misconstrued it as "The kingdom of God is within you," this indicating that the kingdom is an inner experience among Christ's followers whereas it refers to Jesus' presence as the kingdom-bearer. Undoubtedly the RSV translation is the more accurate, but I doubt that the meaning is changed so radically. There are many passages elsewhere in which Jesus calls his followers to enter the kingdom in the present, and these suggest an inward spiritual change. We found them repeatedly in the parables, and they appear elsewhere, twice with a specific reference to the kingdom in the Beatitudes (Matt. 5:3, 10), in the injunction of Matthew 6:33 to "seek first his [God's] kingdom and his righteousness," in the linkage of entrance to the kingdom with doing the will of the Father in Matthew 7:21, in the striking hyperbole of the rich man, the camel, and the needle's eye in Matthew 19:23, 24. One of the very few references in John to the kingdom is that in which Jesus says to Nicodemus, "Truly, truly, I say to you, unless one is born anew, he cannot see the kingdom of God" (3:5).

With this profusion of evidence, with the passages consistent with Jesus' primary message and too many of them to be likely to be due to false reporting, I do not hesitate to regard entrance into the kingdom as a present fact in the life of the Christian, provided the requirements of entrance and life in the kingdom are met. But this is a large proviso which requires some describing.

What does it mean in our time to enter the kingdom of God? It cannot mean moral perfection, for no person has it. It cannot mean sinlessness in the community of Christ's followers, the church, for all the churches are made up of finite, fallible, and sinning persons even though some of these may be saints. Even if it is held that Christ's true church, "the mystical Body of Christ," is sinless, there is no existing, visible church of which this can be said.[13] It cannot mean any existing segment of society, for while some, at least to human eyes, seem nearer the kingdom than others, none is without flaw or fully Christlike.

But the case is not hopeless. To enter the kingdom of God the Christian way is to make such a commitment to Christ that, by the grace of God that has come to us in Christ and the pattern of life put before us by Jesus, life is transformed. This has occurred in vast numbers of people, and at least in some of them the fruits are so visible that there can be no doubt about the fact of life being transformed.

Love is the central requirement of Christian living. "Love bears all things, believes all things, hopes all things, endures all things," says Paul. It is not required of Christian love to bear all things when evil ought to be resisted, or to believe all things when false ideas, beliefs, or rumors are circulated. Yet to bear rather than strike back in anger or hate, to believe rather than engage in groundless suspicion or attack, to hope rather than give in to despair, to endure rather than surrender to difficult circumstances—these are requirements that test the Christian's commitment. Our lives have been blest by people who to a high degree meet these requirements, and such persons are the clearest witness to the meaning of the kingdom of God in our time.

To enter the kingdom as a follower of Christ is to find through the Holy Spirit wisdom, strength, and guidance for living; comfort in sorrow; hope in adversity; outreach in service to others; and an abiding sense of the forgiving and sustaining presence of God. It requires of us penitence, trust, and resolute endeavor. Though it is not without effort on the human side, it is not due to a manipulation of feelings or to good works, but to the grace of God accepted in grateful fidelity.

This is personal religion. But it must not stop with the individual or his immediate surroundings. It must fruit in action to challenge and overcome the evils of society with its poverty, ignorance and disease, its wars and destructive conflicts, its prejudice, oppression, chicanery and quest for profit and power, its insensitivity to the deep needs of persons. Though the power of each individual to remedy these gigantic evils is limited, there is something everybody can do. The first requirement is to avoid contributing to them. A second is to "stand up and be counted" for one's convictions, and thus help to mold public opinion toward a more just and humane society.

The kingdom of God in the present, as I have tried to outline it in consistency with the message of Jesus, could make a great difference in our churches, and through them in society, if it were taken more seriously. It could go far toward overcoming the polarizations that have been cited. It could overcome the debilitating chasm between personal and social religion. It could make evangelism the central concern that it ought to be in any church, but far more than an appeal to sign a card, come forward in a meeting, or become in an external sense a church member. It could make the current interest in the Holy Spirit, long overdue, a life-transforming matter with the manifestation of the fruits of the Holy Spirit in all of life. It could supply the hunger of the soul for spiritual disciplines without having to turn to the Eastern religions. It could immensely further the renewal of the churches, whether in worship or in many other matters, by injecting a new spirit, and this could alleviate the need to look for new gimmicks to make the churches relevant to the modern age. Deep-rooted Christian experience, which is what the kingdom of God in the present essentially means, is relevant to any period in time.

We must look now at the kingdom of God in the future, which is the most difficult and divisive of the three approaches that we are considering. The first thing to be said is that we cannot speak about it with precision, for it is a matter of the ultimate, and our finite minds cannot penetrate the ultimate. Paul said it for us when he wrote, "Eye hath not seen, nor ear heard, neither have entered into the heart of man, the things which God hath prepared for them that love him" (I Cor. 2:9 KJV). He then says that God has revealed them to us by the Spirit. I take this to mean that through the Spirit we know enough for hope and trust and victorious living, which is all we really need to know. But it still remains true that "we see in a mirror dimly" within this human earthbound scene.

Yet our minds can form a judgment of the path to be followed in arriving at our limited knowledge of the future kingdom. The principal paths that have been followed are an apocalyptic, cataclysmic, second coming to put an end to the present world and the prophetic or social gospel kingdom that has accented the conquest of earth's evil by human effort to increase love and justice in response to God's call. These have been discussed earlier but need to be evaluated further in the light of the contemporary situation.

In chapter 3 I stated several reasons why I find difficulty in the apocalyptic view, though it needs to be reemphasized that one may have an eschatology that is not apocalyptic. To summarize, to literalize the apocalyptic passages in the New Testament, is to run counter to all we know of astronomy and the world of space; they are tied in with the then-current Jewish eschatology and Persian dualism which saw evil in command of creation; as commonly accepted, they encourage passivity about the evils of the present world; they emphasize only one side of the message of Jesus to the exclusion of essential elements; they are grounded at least in part on a misconstruction of biblical poetry and drama. I believe these to be persuasive considerations and have illustrated their effects earlier in this chapter by citing some forms of contemporary adventism.

Yet I respond with my whole being to Handel's *Messiah* and especially to its "Hallelujah Chorus," the most stirring piece of music ever composed. It is not by accident that to listen to it is to bring us to our feet! In the language of inspired imagination that speaks in the present but foresees by faith the future we too can say with the seer of Patmos:

Hallelujah! For the Lord God omnipotent reigneth.

The kingdom of this world is become the kingdom of our Lord and of his Christ; and he shall reign for ever and ever.

King of kings, and Lord of lords. Hallelujah! (Rev. 19:6; 11:15; 19:16).

This I believe to the point of certainty. But I do not attempt to define its nature. To do so would be human presumption, perhaps blasphemy. Were I to attempt it, the vision would fade away.

This points to a crucial aspect of the matter that often becomes blurred in discussion of it. The return of Christ is not identical with the coming of the kingdom. The closing words of Matthew's Gospel are, "Lo, I am with you always, to the close of the age." As the risen and living Christ, the promised Comforter, Advocate and Helper, Jesus Christ is *here*. He is with us and will be to the end of time. He needs only to be welcomed into human lives and his message made regnant in the world's affairs.

So I align myself more nearly with the social gospel kingdom. But I do not go along fully with the earlier forms of it. That view moved in the right direction but was in trouble at a deeper level. When it did not fall into a secular utopianism, which its most discerning Christian exponents never did, it nevertheless tended to rely too much on human effort and not to lay enough stress on divine grace for the conquest of evil. It needed the counter-challenge which neo-orthodoxy brought to it, even as the latter needed in turn to be reminded that it was underestimating what human nature could be and do when put at the disposal of God.

As events have developed since the waning of both the older liberalism and of neo-orthodoxy, the state of society has moved in opposite directions. What is accented most is the growth of international conflict and domestic tension, crime and immorality, economic instability, personal tension and rootlessness, and withal a deep despair—in short, the arrival of "future shock." Were neo-orthodoxy still around, it would have plenty of evidence to refute what it viewed as the overly optimistic assumptions of liberalism. However, the trek has been to new forms of atheism or humanism, to adventism, and to a substitution of the occult and of Eastern forms of meditation for Christian worship.

But the picture has another side. As was suggested earlier, those born near the turn of the century have seen within it amazing advances—not only in science, technology, and increased knowledge, but in the conquest of disease with the prolongation of life, an increase in the recognition of race and sex equality with accompanying legal steps; manifold ministries of welfare to the poor, the young, and the elderly; a growing concern for civil rights in many of its facets. To these developments here may be added abroad the retreat of colonialism and the advance of developing nations toward autonomy and importance in the world scene. All this might be summed up by saying that we have a far greater sense of the dignity and worth of personhood than was present in any earlier day.

Is the world getting better or worse? Sociologically, this is a futile question, for there have been great changes in both directions. What one accents will depend on one's own experiences, temperament, and general outlook on the world. Neither assured progress nor disruptive decay is fully in evidence.

What one can say in the midst of a complex and changing world is that it is still God's world, and God is still working for good within it. The process theology is the most promising theological current of our time, and it does not claim that all process is progress. Continuous creation must take place at times against heavy odds. Yet with Professor A. N. Whitehead it believes in God as working through "the tender elements of the world, which slowly and in quietness operate by love." [14] I accept this view though not on the basis of Whitehead whom I have never understood very well. I accept it because I believe it to be in keeping with the picture and message of Jesus that I find in the New Testament.

If anyone is concerned to label my theological position, I have always considered myself to be an evangelical liberal, and still do. Regardless of labels, I believe that the creating and redeeming God has greater things yet in store for the fulfillment of his purposes upon this planet. The final form his victory over evil will take is not within my province to predict. It is difficult to envisage, because of the depth and power of human sin, that God's kingdom will ever fully come on earth, but I do not rule out the possibility. When we speak of the end, the word can mean either goal or termination, and the goal is what most immediately affects us, provided we can view it with hope. If the victory comes as a new heaven and a new earth, then the best description we can give of it is in the words of scripture, "Behold, the dwelling of God is with men. He will dwell with them, and they shall be his people, and God himself will be with them; he will wipe away every tear from their eyes, and death shall be no more." (Rev. 21:3, 4)

I have not dealt with the death and afterlife of the individual thus far in this book, though I have done so elsewhere at considerable length.[15] The issues involved, though related, are not identical. But the mode of approach is the same. We can trust the loving kindness of God to give us what is best for us and our loved ones in the realm beyond bodily death without an exact description of its nature. We need not abandon hope in eternal life, though we accept it by faith and not by sight. So by faith in the power and the goodness of God as God has come to us in Christ, we can know that our world and our destiny are in God's hands and face the future with hope and anticipation.

VII
Thy Kingdom Come

The previous chapter ended with the affirmation that we can have assurance and hope without precise knowledge of the nature of the final consummation of God's purposes in the coming of the kingdom, even as we can have a similar assurance of the individual's life beyond death. The grounds of this assurance are the same in each case—the love, the goodness, and the adequacy of God. In either field, our position must rest on faith in God, but in conjunction also with the most reasonable conclusions we can draw from such knowledge as we have.

The possibility of drawing some such conclusions is within our grasp. We are not obliged to face a blank wall as we face the future. Assurance falls short of explicit knowledge, but it is not the same as fantasy. In fact, the less we fantasize, the more solidly grounded is our assurance. In this last chapter I shall try to do two things: to trace some connections between the Christian hope of eternal life and the coming of the kingdom; and to indicate the major foundations on which I believe both these forms of faith must rest.

1. The destiny of the individual person

There are two reasons why the future of the individual beyond death needs to be considered in connection with the kingdom of God, even though they are not identical concepts. The first is that it affects us all where we live. Far more important to most persons than any theoretical speculation about the future of humanity is a more immediate question. We all must die. Our loved ones die and leave us grieving in the pain of a great separation. We want to know whether they live on in happiness, and whether we shall ever be reunited. We hope so. The churches have long said so. But appearances are against it, and we wonder.

A second reason for coming to terms with belief in the afterlife stems from the precarious state of human life upon this planet. Until recent years, unless one were an adventist expecting an imminent second coming of Christ, it could be taken for granted that persons would inhabit the earth indefinitely. In some far distant astronomical time, the sun's heat might give out, but that need not worry us now. But no longer is it possible to be so confident. The threat of atomic destruction has hung over the world since 1945. More recently, exhaustion of the earth's natural resources through misuse of the environment and of the world's food supply through overpopulation have become serious possibilities. We do not know how much time is left before human folly, not the fulfillment of God's purposes, may put an end to human existence upon earth. If this occurs, God's rulership will continue in his eternal kingdom, but not among persons on earth. I believe we should confront this possibility without undue alarm but reckon with it.

The kingdom concept is related to that of the individual, but is not identical with it because it is a corporate, and in that sense a social, concept. The kingdom in the Old Testament refers to the future of the chosen people. In the thought of Jesus and the New Testament writers, it is the inclusive body of Christ's followers who have become God's redeemed, obedient, and faithful servants. Thus it soon became identified with the church, and this tendency has persisted in spite of the fact that no visible church fully incorporates it.

Throughout most of the Old Testament period, little was said and apparently little thought about an afterlife for the individual. In Job 19:26 there is a crucial passage which the RSV translates "without my flesh I shall see God," though the KJV says "in my flesh" and other versions give various translations along a different line. The belief in a personal resurrection was developed during the intertestamental period, and we have reflections of it in the reply of Jesus to the Sadducees who did not believe in it and tried to trip him over this issue (Matt. 22:23–33). Jesus apparently accepted it. Among his followers it hinges mainly on Jesus' own resurrection and the many references to it in Paul's letters, especially I Corinthians 15. In these passages the primary note is God's victory over death and the presence of God both in time and eternity.

The Bible is not the only source of belief in an afterlife. It is found in virtually every major religion, though the forms in which it is conceived differ. It has a place also, whether rejected or affirmed, in philosophy. Here there is an approach to the afterlife which is worth considering in conjunction with Christian thought.

Any philosophical discussion of the future life is apt to be related to the conservation of values. This means the preservation of goodness, truth, beauty, and whatever else makes life rich and meaningful in a mature soul. Are these values ephemeral or lasting? Sometimes they are thought to be conserved in the influences we leave in the ongoing stream of life upon this planet. Again they are viewed as contributions to the Absolute, or Over-soul, or God conceived as an impersonal essence or ground of all that exists. It is the Christian view that in a world created and sustained by God values persist, but in a more personal way than either of these routes suggests. The most valuable and meaningful element in all creation is human personality; it is human selves that must be preserved if their values are not to be lost either in the dissolution of the body or some final cataclysm that may destroy our world.

Then what may we believe on the basis of Christian faith about life after death? Our primary ground of confidence is that in God's keeping all is well, both for ourselves and those we love. But we can go a step farther as a deduction from what we know of the present life. God has set us in a network of social relations, very precious to us when these relations are what they ought to be. "God setteth the solitary in families" (Ps. 68:6 KJV)—families of blood kinship, of congeniality of heart and soul, and in the broadest sense, of the family of man. These relationships can become warped and too often do, but at their best and truest they are God's most precious gifts. It can hardly be supposed that a loving God would permit these relationships to be ended forever by the death of the body, lonely though the separation may be during the intervening years.

Again, in this life of the earthly pilgrimage, God gives us work to do according to our gifts and capacities. Work also is a great gift, not simply as a means of meeting material needs and caring for those we love, but as a source of self-fulfillment in a meaningful life. Even when bodily strength diminishes, one can still live zestfully and lend strength and cheer to others. Hence, I cannot believe that the life eternal is one of endless idleness. If it were endless duration only, it would be endless boredom and scarcely willed by God. What we may be given to do in the next life we cannot say, and with so many forms of work in this life related to physical existence, it is useless to speculate. But if there is a fellowship of persons, God will give us tasks for their enrichment.

Since in the present life we are bidden to grow in our own personhood, why not in the next? The traditional Protestant view is of sudden sinlessness for the redeemed, with everlasting punishment for the unsaved. The Roman Catholic view more mercifully has purgatory as a preparation for heaven. But instead of either, it may be that we shall continue to grow toward spiritual maturity, never fully achieved in the present life. It would be a welcome opportunity.

And, finally, the life beyond death can be one of joy. Whether we call it resurrection or immortality, our faith holds out this promise. Resurrection with God's gift of a new spiritual body is the major biblical concept (cf. I Cor. 15:42–44, 55–57) though immortality is mentioned a number of times (Rom. 2:7; I Cor. 15:53, 54; II Tim. 1:10). Some insist on speaking of resurrection rather than immortality, lest the latter be construed as a Greek concept of an immortal soul that is separable from a perishing body. In any case, freedom from the present body can be an introduction into joy for the aged or terminally ill when life has run its course. But a far greater happiness for all may be envisioned in God's nearer presence and fellowship with those we love, the preservation of all that is best and finest in the values knit into the self in one's earth life, work to do for others and growth in grace, knowledge, and love.

Such a projection of future possibilities for the individual after bodily death is a matter of faith rather than something finite minds can affirm as if we had the wisdom of God. God may have other and better things in store for us, for "it does not yet appear what we shall be." Yet I believe these projections to be more than fantasy. At any rate, I believe them to be rooted not only in Scripture but in the nature of God, in the nature of human personality, and in the relations of persons to one another as we know them now.

2. The coming kingdom

Having stated what I believe can be said with some assurance about the future of the individual beyond death, I turn now to the main theme of this book for some concluding words. It may be helpful to observe similarities as well as differences between these two contexts of the future.

In the previous chapter I have already stated that I do not think it lies within human knowledge to say whether God's final victory over evil and the final consummation of his kingdom will come within human history or beyond it. Should the end be precipitated by human agencies in defiance of the will of God, it would obviously need to come in a realm beyond human existence on this earth. But should events continue in their normal course, with the ups and downs of human history and a forward movement that prevails in spite of temporary regressions, the future is open.

About a century ago, the poet Alfred Tennyson wrote:

> One God, one law, one element,
> And one far-off divine event,
> To which the whole creation moves.

I do not think this necessarily implies utopianism unless "the whole creation" is interpreted atomistically to mean that everything that looks evil is actually good. I am willing to accept it as a true statement of a purposeful, forward movement without defining the terminus. In general, the exponents of process theology of the Whitehead school stop short of affirming an ultimate end of the world process, while Teilhard de Chardin found it in the Omega Point with Christ as the goal of the evolutionary process. Moltmann and Pannenberg, the leading exponents of the theology of hope, make less of social evolution but believe that Christians are summoned to action in society by the promise of an eschatological future. I shall not attempt to choose among these positions, but will try to say what I believe we can be reasonably sure of.

In the first place, the kingdom of God is present wherever

human beings love and serve God and seek in obedience to extend acceptance of his kingly reign upon earth. The kingdom-as-recognized is not always identical with the kingdom-as-existing. It was present in the Old Testament period before Jesus made it his central message; it is present in the worship and moral endeavors of those of faiths other than Christianity; in acts and attitudes of compassion and a determined effort to bring about a better world, it may be present in persons of no acknowledged religious faith. We enter it at any point in time through the power released and the pattern and promise set forth by Jesus. In this sense it is essentially a Christian doctrine, but this does not preclude the fact that others than Christians may experience its power and contribute toward its forward movement within human affairs.

In a somewhat more specific sense, the concept of the kingdom as both present and future has a correlate in the concept of eternal life presented in John's Gospel. One enters eternal life where he is in the present and by becoming a believer in Christ—a believer not only in the mind but in the commitment of life. It is not by accident that John 3:16 has become, world wide, the most beloved and familiar single verse in the Bible. It is by believing, which means by being born anew, that one enters the kingdom of God (John 3:3, 5). This is equivalent to saying that one enters into eternal life. This does not rule out eternal life after death, for in John 14:1–3 we find some of the greatest words on this theme in all literature. But it is significant that this Gospel puts its emphasis, not on Christ's return as the Son of man, but on the coming of the Holy Spirit as a living presence to replace the bodily presence of Jesus.

The presence of the kingdom is attested by Paul, and he seems to equate it with a term he uses much more frequently, to be "in Christ." "The kingdom of God," he says, "does not mean food and drink but righteousness and peace and joy in the Holy

154

Spirit'' (Rom. 14:17)—an admirable definition of its major marks. Elsewhere he says pungently, ''For the kingdom of God does not consist in talk but in power'' (I Cor. 4:20). In other passages he speaks of ''inheriting'' the kingdom of God, but still with an emphasis on its moral requirements that must be met (I Cor. 6:9, 10; 15:50; Gal. 5:21). This points toward the future, but with the seat of its obligations in the present.

What this brings us to is the fact that ''Thy kingdom come'' is for the present as well as the future and needs to be so understood in reference to the whole of Christian living. But what of the kingdom as future? And how does it correlate with the hope of life after death for the individual?

I have said that the hope of existence beyond bodily death is a form of belief in the conservation of values. This is to say that human life, in spite of its suffering, turmoil, and sometimes its apparent aimlessness, is still meaningful. In the providence of God, the good persists to be used for further good, even though in the immediate scene it may appear to be lost. These convictions stem from the belief that human personality is so valuable that God conserves it even after death as the bearer of these values.

This conviction is a basic note in the kingdom that is yet to come. The road along the way to a better world, which is to say to the fulfillment of God's purposes, is bound to be a rugged one. Whether or not one believes in a personal devil, there are demonic forces in the world—cruel, sadistic, self-centered, lusting for power at any cost. The principalities and powers of which Paul spoke are with us. They assail the righteous as well as those of evil intent. They induce not only evil-doing but loss of hope. In their tug at the soul of man, they induce despair. Only by faith in the goodness of God and his power to conserve the good and even at times to make good come out of evil, can courage and the forward look be maintained.

In the presence of such forces, which seem to be more evident at some periods of history than others, it is easy to give up believing in either the goodness of life or the goodness of God. The quest then to enjoy superficial pleasures and to seize what one can for one's self supplants a more stable and hopeful existence. We seem to be in one of these periods at present.

The Christian concept of the coming kingdom of God runs counter to this mood of pessimism and redeems it through hope. Without overlooking the evil, it affirms that this is still God's world, that God is working within it for good in spite of the evil that thwarts his purposes, and that God conserves in his own ways, often hidden from us, whatever of good we put into it. As individuals, whatever he may have in store for us in the afterlife, on earth we shall soon be forgotten, so transient is human recollection. But by faith we can know that whatever we do wisely and faithfully at God's call will endure.

I suggested also that from what we know of social relations in this life, the next life will be a society of persons in which the ties of love will be preserved. This we can believe also about the coming kingdom. To inherit the kingdom has an important meaning probably not intended by Paul, for its content includes past as well as future. We have inherited from the past vast amounts of good in physical sustenance, knowledge, works of beauty, sensitivity to spiritual insights, the culture that has come to us from a long past, and, not least, our Christian faith. It is reasonable to expect that, barring the holocaust, future ages will inherit these same values from us plus, we hope, some accretions from our own time. To pray "Thy kingdom come" is to pray in vital expectancy that these legacies will be carried forward in a greater doing of God's will on earth.

This will not happen automatically. To pray for the coming of God's kingdom without working for it is laziness and lethargy. Furthermore, it is blasphemy. The three petitions at the beginning of the Lord's prayer all hang together. "Hallowed be thy name" means "In reverence, give God glory." "Thy will be done on earth, as it is in heaven" means "In fidelity, give God labor." Paul's word that "the kingdom of God does not consist in talk but in power" is nowhere better illustrated than in the repetition of prayer for the coming of God's kingdom without comparable effort that God's will should be done on earth.

The goal of the kingdom, both for the immediate and the long-range future, is again aptly summed up by Paul when he speaks of it as "righteousness and peace and joy in the Holy Spirit." This is an inspired combination of terms, for they embody the goals of the kingdom, both as personal living and as the new society of the future for which we labor and pray. With a word about each of these great themes we conclude this study.

Righteousness is not a matter of ethics only, but of Christian faith at its foundations. A good God demands goodness in his people. It is a demand that appears throughout the Bible, coming to its climax in the message and ministry of Jesus and his call to love. There are differences of opinion as to the forms of action required by righteousness, and some objections to the word as suggesting a rigid legalism, but little dispute about righteousness as an essential mark of life in the kingdom of God.

However, there is dispute—and a large one—over the unrighteous and what God does with the unrepentant sinner. Traditional faith has said that he is cast into hell, not simply the vague and shadowy Sheol of the Old Testament but to Christian literalists, a burning lake of fire to suffer eternally. Others of us are obliged to believe that this is inconsistent with the character of God. It is something that no morally sensitive human being would do, to say nothing of a God of love. The fact that there are such passages in the New Testament, drawn from Jewish apocalypticism and attributed to Jesus, does not prove that he said them or that he could have believed this to be an appropriate fate. But if we renounce belief in such a hell, must we renounce judgment also? I think not. Judgment comes, we know, in the natural course of events on those who defy the physical, the moral, or the spiritual laws of God. There is deep truth in the belief that whatsoever a man—or a society—sows, that will be reaped. Judgment comes also in an inner deterioration of personality, and while psychiatrists may not wish to speak of sin, they must deal with its effects. Along with such visible manifestations of judgment there is that condemnation in love which has traditionally been called the wrath of God. This means that God takes sin seriously, and such condemnation may fall upon us, even in a professed state of righteousness, for our injustice, our indifference to human needs, or any other sin against the love commandment.

Peace—how we yearn for it! And how much it is needed in our time, among the nations, between clashing economic or political groups, in families, in personal relations of all kinds. Conflict can sometimes be creative, but hostility is a breeder of many types of sin. No wonder that in spite of continuing warfare, which has grown to colossal proportions with ever more deadly weapons, Christ is still designated as the Prince of Peace. As was foreseen by prophets of old, with the coming of God's kingdom there would be no more war.

In other fields as well, the drawing together of persons in a closer unity of spirit in spite of diversity of cultures and opinions may well be a fundamental note in the coming of the kingdom. Some evidences of this, in spite of problems still to be resolved, may be seen in the birth of both the ecumenical movement and the United Nations in our time. Much more needs to be done before we are "one in the Spirit" in either church or society.

The third note that Paul links with righteousness and peace is joy in the Spirit. This we saw to be a basic note also in a Christian understanding of eternal life. Joy is a legitimate quest of the human spirit, for time or for eternity. It is one of the greatest gifts of God. It is available for the taking, if we will meet the other requirements of the kingdom.

There are many ways of saying this. None surpasses Paul's paean of victory at the end of the eighth chapter of Romans. "Who shall separate us from the love of Christ?" The things he enumerates are abroad in our world today. Then comes the answer, "No, in all these things we are more than conquerors through him who loved us." If we believe this, we can believe in the kingdom of God as both present and future; we can work for it as we wait for it; and we can know that our times and our lives are in God's hands.

Notes

Chapter One   Where We Stand

1. I have included some further discussion of the Jesus movement in my *Mysticism: Its Meaning and Message* (Nashville: Abingdon Press, 1973), pp. 174–77.
2. "The Six Greatest Men of History," *American Magazine*, November, 1922.
3. Cf. Henry J. Cadbury, *The Peril of Modernizing Jesus* (New York: The Macmillan Co., 1937).
4. These words are attributed to the returning nobleman in the parable of the pounds (Luke 19:11–27). However, its setting, as of the similar parable of the talents in Matthew 25:14–30, is divine judgment at Christ's return.
5. Frederick C. Grant, *The Gospel of the Kingdom* (New York: The Macmillan Co., 1940), pp. x–xi.
6. The popularity of this movement is evidenced by the attention given to it in the secular press when assemblies of its adherents attract thousands in attendance.
7. In addition to the major affirmations in the chapters indicated, the second coming of Christ or the Son of man is directly affirmed in Matt. 10:23; Mark 8:38 and 14:62; Luke 12:40, 18:8, and 23:42; and John 21:22. It is implied and less decisively stated in Matt. 13:41; Mark 10:37; Luke 12:8-9, 13:35, and 22:29-30; John 14:3, 18, 28, 16:16. The book of Acts affirms a second coming in 1:11 and 3:20-21 though it is silent about it thereafter. The letters, whether of Paul or others, abound in such passages. See I Cor. 4:5, 11:26, and 16:22; II Cor. 5:10; I Thess. 1:10 and 4:15-17; Heb. 9:28; Jas. 5:8-9. In numerous other passages there is an oblique reference which may or may not be thus interpreted.

Chapter Two   The Spectrum of Opinion

1. Johannes Weiss, *Jesus' Proclamation of the Kingdom of God,* trans. and ed. Richard H. Hiers and D. Larrimore Holland (Philadelphia: Fortress Press, 1971).
2. Albert Schweitzer, *The Mystery of the Kingdom of God: The Secret of Jesus' Messiahship and Passion,* trans. Walter Lowrie (New York: The Macmillan Co., 1950).
3. Albert Schweitzer, *The Quest of the Historical Jesus: A Critical Study of Its Progress from Reimarus to Wrede,* 3rd ed., new introduction by author (New York: The Macmillan Co., 1968).
4. Cf. James M. Robinson, *The New Quest of the Historical Jesus* (Naperville, Ill.: Allenson, 1959). Deals with the modern stance of apocalyptic eschatology in contemporary New Testament interpretation and especially with Bultmann's position.
5. Günther Bornkamm, *Jesus of Nazareth,* trans. Irene and Fraser McLuskey with James M. Robinson (New York: Harper & Row, 1961), p.13. This life of Jesus rests on a considerably revised basis from those produced in the nineteenth century or in the early part of the twentieth.
6. Schweitzer, *The Quest of the Historical Jesus,* p. 238.
7. *Ibid.,* p. 401.
8. Albert Schweitzer, *The Mysticism of Paul the Apostle* (New York: The Macmillan Co., 1955).
9. *Ibid.,* p. 384.
10. Norman Perrin, *The Kingdom of God in the Teaching of Jesus* (Philadelphia: The Westminster Press, 1963), pp. 32–34.
11. Walter Rauschenbush, *A Theology for the Social Gospel* (New York: The Macmillan Co., 1917).
12. L. Harold DeWolf, *A Theology of the Living Church,* rev. ed. (New York: Harper and Row, 1960).
13. George Eldon Ladd, *Jesus and the Kingdom* (New York: Harper & Row, 1964), pp. 11–13.
14. Perrin, *The Kingdom of God in the Teaching of Jesus,* pp. 148–57.
15. Frederick C. Grant, *The Gospel of the Kingdom* (New York: The Macmillan Co., 1940), pp. 63, 67, 153, 156.
16. *Ibid,* p. 137.
17. DeWolf, *A Theology of the Living Church,* pp. 306-314.
18. Charles H. Dodd, *The Parables of the Kingdom,* rev. ed. (New York: Charles Scribner's Sons, 1938).
19. Dodd, *The Parables of the Kingdom,* p. 106.
20. *Ibid.,* p. 49.
21. *Ibid,* p. 109.
22. I am using this designation instead of "existential eschatology" because the

latter is an ambiguous term which one tends to apply to any point of view which he considers the right one.

23. Rudolf Bultmann, *Theology of the New Testament*, vol. 1, trans. Kendrick Grobel (New York: Charles Scribner's Sons, 1970), pp. 24, 11–12. See also Bultmann, *Jesus and the Word*, trans. Louise Pettibone Smith and Erminie Huntress (New York: Charles Scribner's Sons, 1934), pp. 72 ff.

24. Bultmann's view is that Jesus regarded his own work as the "sign of the time," but did not think of himself as either the Messianic king or the supernatural Son of man. *Theology of the New Testament*, vol. 1, pp. 8, 27–34.

Chapter Three   What Is the Kingdom of God?

1. These points of general agreement are presented, though slightly differently, in chapter 5, "The Kingdom of God," in my earlier book, *Our Christian Hope* (Nashville: Abingdon Press, 1964).

2. Grant, *The Gospel of the Kingdom*, pp. 63, 67, 153, 156.

3. See S. E. Johnson in *The Interpreter's Dictionary of the Bible*, vol. R–Z (Nashville: Abingdon Press, 1962), pp. 413–16 for an extensive and detailed presentation of the use of the term "Son of man" in the Old Testament, in the Synoptic Gospels, and in John. What emerges from this study is that Jesus in the Synoptics appears to use the term in three senses: in reference to his own earthly mission; as the transcendent one as in Enoch but without definite self-designation; and as the latter referring to himself. In John's Gospel the most distinctive contribution is that the pre-existent Son of man, who has come down from heaven and given life to the world, will ascend again.

4. *The World Mission of the Church* (London and New York: International Missionary Council, 1939), p. 106.

5. In outlining the three principal meanings attached to the term "kingdom of God," I am heavily indebted to John Knox for his *Christ the Lord: The Meaning of Jesus in the Early Church* (Chicago: Willett, Clark and Co., 1945), pp. 24–30.

Chapter Four   The Kingdom Before and After Jesus

1. The doctrine of the remnant, having passed through the crucible and reinterpretations of New Testament thought, still persists in the belief of Jehovah's Witnesses and other Pentecostals that on the day of the second coming, they alone will be taken to dwell with Jesus in heaven.

2. Quoted by O. E. Evans in *The Interpreter's Dictionary of the Bible*, K–Q (Nashville: Abingdon Press, 1962), p. 19.

3. John Bright, *The Kingdom of God* (Nashville: Abingdon Press, 1953).

Chapter 6 uses the suggestive term "the holy commonwealth" to designate this aspect of the outlook of Judaism.

4. It is the contention of S. G. F. Brandon in *Jesus and the Zealots: A Study of the Political Factor in Primitive Christianity* (New York: Charles Scribner's Sons, 1968) that Jesus was a Zealot and a violent exponent of nationalism. This position has been effectively answered by George R. Edwards in *Jesus and the Politics of Violence* (New York: Harper and Row, 1972).

5. John Knox in *Christ the Lord*, pp. 30–38, points out Jesus probably used the terms "Son of man" in both senses, but that the early church, convinced that he was the Messiah, gave an eschatological interpretation to some sayings not so intended. He gives a more extended list of such passages.

6. John Bright, *The Kingdom of God*, pp. 208–14, regards Jesus as definitely believing himself to be the Messiah, but in the pattern and concept of the Suffering Servant.

7. The affirmation in Mark 14:61 in answer to Pilate's question is less likely to have been spoken by Jesus than the replies given in Matthew 27:11 and Luke 22:70, for if he had said that he was the Son of God, the Jews could have put him to death for blasphemy.

8. There is no single word in English by which to translate the full meaning of the Paraclete. It has been variously rendered as comforter, counselor, advocate, and simply helper.

Chapter Five   The Kingdom in the Parables

1. Joachim Jeremias, *Rediscovering the Parables* (New York: Charles Scribner's Sons, 1966), p. 10.

2. C. H. Dodd, *The Parables of the Kingdom* (New York: Charles Scribner's Sons, 1938), p. 22.

3. Albert E. Barnett, *Understanding the Parables of Our Lord* (Nashville: Abingdon-Cokesbury Press, 1940), p. 63.

4. Dodd says that these parables do not emphasize the value of the kingdom, since Jesus' hearers already knew this, but the sacrifice by which it is acquired. (*Parables of the Kingdom*, p. 112). This seems to me an unwarranted assumption and a false disjunction.

5. Dietrich Bonhoeffer, *The Cost of Discipleship* (New York: The Macmillan Co., 1959), pp. 37-49.

6. Karl Menninger, *Whatever Became of Sin?* (New York: Hawthorn Books, 1973).

7. Morton Smith in *The Secret Gospel: The Discovery and Interpretation of the Secret Gospel According to Mark* (New York: Harper & Row, 1973) endeavors, on the basis of a manuscript fragment believed to be a copy of a

letter from Clement of Alexandria, to prove that Jesus was a magician who taught such a secret gospel. This then becomes "the mystery of the kingdom," with baptism as its initiation rite, and Christianity becomes a mystery religion. This seems to me completely unpersuasive.

8. The allegorical interpretation given in the Gospels makes the point of the parable the different modes of reception of the word of God. Jeremias points out that this gives the parable a psychological slant, whereas its original reference was probably to the harvest at the end of time. Whether the setting is present or future, the parable in either case has to do with one's place in the kingdom. Cf. Joachim Jeremias, *Rediscovering the Parables,* pp. 64, 119 f.

9. *The Parables of the Kingdom,* chapter 5 and especially pp. 171, 174.

Chapter Six   The Difference It Makes

1. *The Modern Rival of Christian Faith* (New York and Nashville: Abingdon-Cokesbury Press, 1952), chapter 6.

2. Stated by Dr. Alan Walker of Sydney, Australia in an address at the School of Theology at Claremont, Nov. 5, 1973.

3. *Awake!* Oct. 8, 1973, p. 31. The United Methodist *Upper Room* is published in more languages, but it is not a news magazine.

4. Nearly 130 million copies of this folder were distributed in 1973, and the placing of another folder in a half billion homes around the world was projected for 1974. *The Watchtower,* Oct. 15, 1973, p. 635.

5. This summary of beliefs is taken from the Oct. 8, 1973 issue of *Awake!* pp. 16–20.

6. Hal Lindsey with C. C. Carlson, *The Late Great Planet Earth* (Grand Rapids: Zondervan Publishing House, 1970). Republished in paperback by Bantam Books. By February, 1973, it had gone through twenty-six printings, and had sold over two million copies.

7. Lindsey, *The Late Great Planet Earth,* p. 162.

8. *Christ—the Hope of the World: Documents on the Main Theme of the Second Assembly.* (Geneva: World Council of Churches, 1954), pp. 13, 11, 12.

9. Jürgen Moltmann, *Theology of Hope: On the Ground and the Implications of a Christian Eschatology,* trans. James W. Leitch (New York: Harper & Row, 1967).

10. Jacques Ellul, *Hope in Time of Abandonment,* trans. C. Edward Hopkin (New York: The Seabury Press, 1973).

11. *The Providence of God* (New York and Nashville: Abingdon Press, 1960.) Republished as *Does God Care?* (Waco, Tex.: Word Books, 1974).

12. Daniel Day Williams, *God's Grace and Man's Hope* (New York: Harper & Row, 1949), p. 197.

13. In ecumenical assemblies, especially the World Council of Churches, it has not been unusual for representatives of the Eastern Orthodox Church to withhold assent on this basis to statements which refer to the church as sinning.
14. Alfred North Whitehead, *Process and Reality* (New York: The Macmillan Co., 1929), p. 520.
15. *Conflicts in Religious Thought*, (New York: Holt, 1929; Harper, 1949), chapter 12; in the following books by the Abindgon Press, *Understanding the Christian Faith*, 1947, chapter 10; *The Providence of God*, 1960, chapter 8; *Our Christian Hope*, 1964, chapter 6; *What Christians Believe*, 1965, chapter 6; and in *Beliefs That Count* (Nashville: Graded Press, 1961), chapter 12.

Scripture Index

Old Testament

Index

Intertestamental Writings

Subject Index